Restaging Feminisms

Elaine Aston

Restaging Feminisms

palgrave
macmillan

Elaine Aston
Lancaster University
Lancaster, UK

ISBN 978-3-030-40588-5 ISBN 978-3-030-40589-2 (eBook)
https://doi.org/10.1007/978-3-030-40589-2

This Palgrave Pivot imprint is published by the registered company Springer Nature Switzerland AG
The registered company address is: Gewerbestrasse 11, 6330 Cham, Switzerland

For my children Magdalene and Daniel, grandchildren William and Leo

Contents

CHAPTER 1

Restaging Feminisms

Abstract This chapter introduces the premise of the study: a re-encounter with the tripartite modelling of liberal, radical and socialist feminisms that were foundational to pioneering feminist approaches to theatre. Past-present feminism and theatre connections are introduced and explored in the context of feminism's significant revival as a social movement. Both the vicissitudes of feminism since the seventies and the shifts in the feminist-theatre landscape are outlined. Part II of the chapter focuses on the legacies and renewals of feminist dynamics within the British theatre industry: the liberal-feminist demand for equality; radical-feminist resistance to sexual harassment in the industry; and the contestation of class and intersectional inequalities.

Keywords Feminisms · Feminist movement · Feminist theatre · Affect · Equality & diversity in British theatre industry

Violet, white and green—these were the suffrage colours resurrected in 2018. On 10 June, thousands of women took to the streets of Belfast (Northern Ireland), Cardiff (Wales), Edinburgh (Scotland) and London (England), participating in a public artwork designed as a nationwide celebration of the centenary year of the Representation of the People Act (1918).[1] As women paraded through the cities, they created a human banner in the suffrage colours: marched in lines banded green, white and violet to commemorate the suffragettes who demanded 'Give Women the

E. Aston, *Restaging Feminisms*,
https://doi.org/10.1007/978-3-030-40589-2_1

Vote'. The marches were theatrical and celebratory; feminism symbolically flowed through the streets of each city. But flying under the human banner of suffrage were notes of contemporary protest: commemorating these past feminist struggles, women also were demonstrating that in today's socially unjust and equality-resistant neoliberal Britain, women's rights are far from achieved. Rather, they still urgently need to be fought for.

Indeed, the age of neoliberal austerity ushered in by the global banking crisis of 2007–2008 has seen entrenched and deepening inequalities. Where the fight for women's suffrage can be claimed as the coming of equality, one hundred years later neoliberal Britain aptly deserves the title of Beatrix Campbell's 2013 manifesto: *End of Equality*. However, when equality is revoked, then, to quote Campbell's subtitle: *The Only Way Is Women's Liberation*. Over the course of the last decade, feminism as a social movement has become more high profile than it has been since its second wave of activism in the seventies. Today's British feminists loudly chorus an end to the centuries-old 'drama' of patriarchy and voice commitments to any number of socially progressive struggles, protests and campaigns. They protest the erosion of women's rights, demand an end to male violence against women and to oppressions formed by the socio-economic arrangements of a neoliberal order. Of course, as the astute, feminist reader will no doubt be quick to point out, none of these concerns are new. They all reverberate with feminist struggles of the seventies and the principal feminisms deployed to address them: from the liberal-feminist strategies to advance women's rights, through radical feminism's protest against the violence perpetrated by patriarchalism, to the socialist-feminist analyses of the material circumstances of women's oppression.

Observing these past-present feminist connections, I also detected a revival of academic interest in second-wave feminism. Previously, in terms of feminist theory, seventies feminism had been widely cast as 'the essentialist decade' (Hemmings 2011: 40) and deemed outmoded in the light of subsequent iterations of feminism that seemingly progressed in a linear fashion from identity politics in the 1980s, through the poststructuralist play of differences in the 1990s, to the adoption of intersectional approaches in the twenty-first century. But the renewed feminist struggles have occasioned a critical (in all senses) recycling of the second wave. Victoria Hesford's *Feeling Women's Liberation* (2013) offers a seminal re-evaluation of the seventies women's liberation movement in the USA that intervenes in how the history of the movement was produced and recorded. Elsewhere, Finn Mackay's *Radical Feminism: Feminist Activism in Movement* (2015) reclaims radical feminism for contemporary British feminist activism. Equally, writing the foreword to the new edition of Michèle Barrett's *Women's Oppression Today*, Kathi Weeks concludes: 'I would like to consider it an open question whether the *Today* of the book's title refers only to 1980 or if it could also refer to other times, even some that are yet to come' (2014: xix).

Restaging Feminisms is inspired by this critical turn to feminism's past—by the reassessment of seventies feminism as insightful to the urgency of 'feeling women's liberation' in today's climate of anti-democratic neoliberalism. Specifically, I propose a re-encounter with the tripartite modelling of liberal, radical and socialist feminisms that proved foundational to pioneering feminist approaches to theatre. Political understanding and application of the principal feminisms was seminal to what Sue-Ellen Case outlined in her groundbreaking *Feminism and Theatre* as the necessity of finding 'ways to evaluate theatre work from within feminist politics' and to understanding the 'connection between the social [feminist] movement and the stage' (2008 [1988]: 2). Thus, revisiting the feminisms, I set out to explore the criticality, aesthetics and affective strategies of performances that variously recycle, reclaim or renew liberal-, radical- and socialist-feminist dynamics. In short, three decades after Case's landmark publication, *Restaging Feminisms* re-opens the forensic examination of the feminisms, their renewed relevance to the feminist movement and resonance on the contemporary British stage.

Part I: Reviewing Feminism and Theatre

'The Hard Road to [Feminism's] Renewal'

Booking-ending Case's *Feminism and Theatre* with *Restaging Feminisms* necessarily invites the question of what happened to feminism in between times. To put this another way: it calls for consideration as to why, prior to the last decade, feminism as a political movement did not gain traction. Why was it such a 'hard road to renewal'?

My signposting of Stuart Hall's *The Hard Road to Renewal: Thatcherism and the Crisis of the Left* (1988), gestures to Margaret Thatcher's neoliberal doctrine that she was determined to make hegemonic—politically, ideologically and economically. The 'swing to the right' (Hall 1988: 39), with its neoliberal economics, creed of competitive individualism and the erosion of social welfare, produced the 'crisis' faced by all left-orientated movements, feminism included. Unable to make the political pendulum swing in the opposite direction, at governmental level the Labour Party was left in disarray. Moreover, it was not only the rise of the right that dismantled the Labour-left, but also the left's inability to realign with social movements such as feminism. As Hall puts it in Gramscian terms, this was a failure to grasp how 'the struggle to "remake society" has to be fought as a war of position, conducted on many different fronts at once' (ibid.: 249). Equally, alongside this, the feminist 'front' was also in difficulty. As Joni Lovenduski and Vicky Randall explain, the rise of identity politics in the eighties made it 'clear that the finely balanced tentative democracy of the WLM could not contain the identities that competed for attention' (1993: 88). The category 'women' could no longer function as a signifier of feminism's 'tentative democracy': the recognition of multiple competing identities (of race, class, or sexuality) dismantled the 'basic premiss of feminism, that all women share some common political interests' (ibid.: 89).

Going into the nineties without 'common political interests' left the British feminist movement fragmented. As such, it differed from the situation in North America where a third wave of feminism had more 'popular purchase' (Evans 2015: 3), albeit in a variety of often contradictory ways, ranging from conservatives such as Katie Roiphe or Naomi Wolf to radical third wavers who set a multiracial agenda (Heywood and Drake 1997). Contrastingly, coming out of the anti-feminist backlash of the Thatcherite eighties, British feminism proved susceptible to the sociocultural mainstreaming of post-feminism—'posting' tactics designed to outmanoeuvre feminist claims to the unfinished histories of equality. As Angela McRobbie explains, also in a Gramscian-informed analysis, 'disarticulating feminism' served to rearticulate a 'new kind of regime of gender power', one aimed 'to foreclose on the possibility or likelihood of various expansive intersections and inter-generational feminist transmissions' (2009: 25–26). This strategic dismantling of feminism's capacity to make connections across oppressed citizenries, either as a social movement or by grouping with other social movements, ceded the collectivist feminist terrain to a 'regime' of individualistically styled sense of empowerment and entitlement. Moreover, the election of a Labour government in 1997 that presented an opportunity to reverse this trend and dismantle the neoliberal project proved a missed opportunity: Tony Blair's *New* Labour administration moved increasingly to the centre (if not to the right) dismantling former Labour attachments and articulating a 'Third Way', centrist, 'beyond left and right' position (Seymour 2016: 145). Blair's government deradicalised the social-democratic grammar of the left by adopting neoliberal rhetoric: meritocracy not equality, 'workfare' not welfare and 'reform' coupled with economic 'efficiency' rather than social progress (ibid.: 145, 151). In-keeping with the vision of New Labour, the third-way 'regime of gender power' dismantled attachments to equality struggles thereby leaving the neoliberal project and its patriarchal remains uncontested.

New Labour with its third-way strategies did not survive the global banking crisis. In its place came the austerity-driven economics of David Cameron's Coalition and subsequent Conservative governments. To sell his vision of the 'Big Society' and to dispel the idea of neoliberal capitalism as a bankrupt economic system, Cameron vaunted his slogan: 'we are all in this together' (2010). If '*we* are all in this together', then it follows that nobody can be against 'this': there is no 'us' and 'them' divide. But the severity of inequalities re-marked the historic divide between a wealthy elite and economic disenfranchisement of the masses, now extending to less affluent middle-class sectors. Moreover, Cameron's 'Big Society' was predicated on social exclusion, not an inclusive togetherness, as evinced in the increasing demonisation of the underclass (Jones 2011) and all other social undesirables, cast out as 'revolting subjects' (Tyler 2013). Thus, in a society not big enough to accommodate and care for those disadvantaged by its illiberal system, opposition began to emerge among disenfranchised citizenries: student protests over tuition fees and cuts to further education (2010); public-sector strikes against pension cuts (2011); and nationwide rioting by those adversely affected by austerity measures (2011).

Economic hardship escalated for ordinary women and men, though it was women who bore the brunt of austerity-induced privation (Armstrong 2017), with increasing numbers of women and children in low-income families living below the poverty line (Lansley and Mack 2015). Instead of a benign and caring state, those in urgent need found themselves struggling with the neoliberal belief in the autonomous, self-supporting individual—an ideology that sanctioned the withdrawal of state-subsidised systems of welfare. Equally harmful to women's welfare was a resurgent patriarchalism that was every bit as deadly as its neoliberal counterpart. As the one systematically feeds off and supports the other, this en*genders* a raft of inequalities, a conjunction that Campbell terms a 'neopatriarchal and neoliberal matrix' (2013: 91). Given the rise of a neoliberal neopatriarchy, women—especially among younger generations—began to recognise the idea of gender power for what it really was: an empty, broken promise. By 2013, as *Guardian* journalist Kira Cochrane describes, there were any number of feminist campaigns and protests formed around equality and social issues, notably demands for equal pay, racial equality and an end to the neopatriarchal regime of sexism, sexual harassment and domestic abuse (Cochrane 2013). In short, feminist opposition to the 'end of equality' multiplied and gathered significant momentum.

Furthermore, despite the 'white feminist pushback against intersectionality' on the part of influential voices in the press and media as Reni Eddo-Lodge rightly indicts and highlights (2018 [2017]: 165), at a grass-roots level, today's young generation of UK, feminist activists tend to identify as intersectional feminists (Cochrane 2013). Inspired by US critical race theorist Kimberlé Crenshaw, who proposed the term to explain the law's double discrimination against black women (Crenshaw 1989), the concept of intersectionality circulates among these campaigners as a conceptual prism through which to view the multiple factors that combine to produce differentiated levels of inequality and injustice among women. Hence, while there is much academic debate about the precise meaning and application of the term (Davis 2008), it can readily be grasped as a counter to a gender-only, exclusionary approach. Understood as such, it helps to overcome the kinds of erstwhile divides within the women's liberation movement that were occasioned by identity politics. As one of the black-feminist activists interviewed by Cochrane puts it, at its most fundamental level, understanding how race and gender intersect overcomes the pressure to 'pick a side' (qtd. in Cochrane 2013).

Looking back, the pressure to 'pick a side' often arose whenever feminism was constructed as a linear, unidirectional narrative in which old paradigms were succeeded and displaced by new ones, or when one generational wave was posited as being succeeded by another. Thus, the tendency was to negate sideways patterns of recognition—the laterally woven linkages between past-present thinking. Or, it fostered antagonisms between older and younger generations of feminists who seemingly appeared to be on opposite sides. In truth, sides and divides have been numerous, from the anxiety of choosing the 'correct' theory side[2] to divisions between feminist praxis in the academy and grass-roots activism. Selecting a feminist-political position was no exception. As Lovenduski and Randall observe of second-wave British feminism, the question of which 'appropriate feminist political strategy' to adopt was a matter of 'dispute between feminists' (1993: 7). For radical feminists, the key stratagem was to focus on the power relations that positioned women as a subordinate category to men, thus positing patriarchy as the obstacle to be addressed in the interests of women's empowerment. This was not acceptable to socialist feminists whose attachments to class politics interacted with, if not superseded, sexual politics. Despite these differences, which over time evolved in less disputatious, more synergetic ways, both feminist positions aspired to structural transformations of society: the prioritisation of ending patriarchal domination in the case of radical feminism; the demise of capitalism as a socially unjust system that relied on the exploitation of women's dual productive and reproductive labour, as the basis for socialist feminism. This placed radical and socialist feminisms at odds with the reformist strategies of liberal feminists who saw women's advancement through extant social systems and institutions as the solution. While relatively few women identified as liberal feminists, many adopted 'liberal feminist goals' (ibid.). Thus, in a British context, it makes sense for liberal feminism to be 'better understood as a strategy rather than a movement' (ibid.).

Revisiting Feminist Stages, Rehearsing Methodologies

During the eighties, as feminist-theatre academics began to adopt the three feminisms to analyse the feminist-political dynamics in women's theatre, there was a gravitational pull towards socialist feminism and a materialist analysis. However, declaring a preference for one feminism did not translate into a wilful disparaging of other feminisms. Seminal studies of feminism and theatre, such as Michelene Wandor's *Understudies* (1981) and *Carry on, Understudies* (1986) in the UK, and Jill Dolan's *The Feminist Spectator as Critic* (2012 [1988]) in the USA, aimed to assess the different feminist dynamics and their staging. Even so, attempts to categorise the feminisms and evaluate their 'performance' were not without criticism. As Dolan notes, her parsing of the three feminisms coupled with an ideological commitment to materialist feminism saw one respondent to her early work protesting: 'Clearly, the third is the only one to go for. Yet can it be that there are only three ways to be a feminist, and two of them are ugly?' (qtd. in Dolan 1988: 10).

Given the vicissitudes of the feminisms over the last three decades, the task of *re*-introducing them is decidedly complex; there were difficult decisions to make about how to re-present them concisely and to explore their dynamics on the British stage. Briefly, assigning each feminism its own 'restaging' chapter, I elected to provide introductory frameworks that review respective histories, founding concepts, objectives or desires. Thereafter, the reanimations and renewals of each feminism in British theatre are explored through accompanying case studies. Adopting a tripartite, chapter structure to explore the past-present connections and evolutions of liberal, radical and socialist feminisms marks the political divides between the feminisms. But the blurring of boundaries will also occur as one feminist stance intersects with or makes demands of another. Also, akin to Wandor and Dolan, I should acknowledge my own feminist-political belief: an enduring commitment to socialist feminism—a bias that I hope does not detract from my conviction that the re-mobilisation of different feminist-political stances and strategies can contribute to feminism's counter-hegemonic opposition to the 'neopatriarchal and neoliberal matrix' and the desire to transform it.

Back in the Thatcherite eighties and the backlash against feminism, the reality was that socialist and radical feminists were cast as the 'ugly' sisters to Cinderella as the heroine of a liberal-feminist drama, or more specifically of the *neoliberal* drama that Thatcher was determined on scripting. Thatcher dramaturgically recast the story of women's advancement into the tale of the high-achieving, individual woman able to transcend her material circumstances—a mythical saga subjected to trenchant critique by Caryl Churchill in her landmark play, *Top Girls*, which premiered in 1982 (see Chapter 4). The ironic twist to Thatcher's top-girl tale was its co-option of liberal-feminist efforts to advance women's equality (principally by legislating for their rights and lobbying for their greater participation in the public sphere), into the neoliberal fantasy of the self-empowered individual. By this account, women had been granted the freedom to choose how to live their lives; feminism's advocacy of women's rights was deemed no longer necessary.

Hence, as Wandor observed, it was the exception rather than the rule for feminist theatre with a 'radical' edge to achieve mainstream (commercial) success (1986: 179). To substantiate her point, Wandor singles out Denise Deegan's play from 1983, *Daisy Pulls it Off*: a rags-to-riches story (poor girl succeeds in a posh school and turns out to have a family fortune) as using 'the margins of the bourgeois feminist dynamic', to create what 'is ultimately a very good Thatcherite play' (ibid.: 180). From a feminist perspective, the phenomenon of a successful 'Thatcherite play' by a woman playwright registers the contradictory pull between the liberal-feminist goal to break through the glass ceiling and the theatrical coupling of femininity and finance as a sign of women's alleged progress. In other words, lobbying for more women to move centre stage fails as a feminist strategy if the glass ceiling cracks only to admit a few successful women who then participate in the self-same values that prop up the masculinist and capitalist imagination.

The political sleight of hand that morphed liberal feminism into feminism's neoliberal, top-girl nemesis has persisted to the extent that some feminists insist that there is only one way forward: to engage in 'anticapitalist feminism' as opposed to a continuance of 'equality opportunity domination' (Arruzza et al. 2019: 4). By the latter, Cinzia Arruzza et al. understand liberal feminism operating 'as a handmaiden of capitalism' in which exploitation continues but overseen by equal numbers of 'ruling-class men and women' (ibid.: 2), whereas the former designates a reinvigorated, expanded mode of socialist feminism. If we are to oust the faux-feminist Cinderella from her leading role to reveal capitalism and patriarchalism as the ugly sisters that benefit a minority of privileged, white women and to move feminism in an anti-capitalist, socially progressive direction as Arruzza et al. demand, then one matter we need to comprehend is how liberal feminism transformed into capitalism's 'handmaiden'.

Mindful of this issue, Chapter 2 briefly historicises the entangled histories of liberalism and feminism to set the scene for two plays—Laura Wade's *Home, I'm Darling* (2018) and Nina Raine's *Consent* (2017)—which restage elements foundational to the liberal-feminist terrain. To be clear, neither play is written *from* a liberal-feminist perspective: each problematises liberal-feminist legacies and strategies. In Wade's case, this involves the satirical undermining of neoliberal choice feminism: her comedic critique of a middle-class woman who chooses to abandon her career and return to the 'darling' doll's house. Raine's *Consent* touches on the long-standing concern of liberal feminism with achieving equality reform in a supposedly gender-neutral legal system. Where Wade pulls feminism out from under the rug of the neoliberal 'handmaiden', Raine demonstrates that equality before the law cannot be achieved without a radical overhaul of the patriarchalism embedded in the system.

In the climate of seventies feminism, an alternative to the liberal-feminist strategy of lobbying for more equal opportunities in theatre was to carve out a space for women-only or women-dominated companies in the margins of the malestream. The formation of women's collectives organised along non-hierarchical, democratic lines—a principle that extended to the staging of works where the ensemble was favoured over the individualistic tradition of the star performer and supporting cast—was important to the development of a vibrant feminist-theatre tradition in British theatre. Companies varied in terms of their political outlook and purpose. For instance, among the most high profile of these groups: Monstrous Regiment formed as a socialist-feminist collective; The Women's Theatre Group was dedicated to making work by for and about women; Siren established as a lesbian-identified company; and Clean Break set up to work with women affected by the criminal justice system.[3] Irrespective of these differences, there was an underlying sense that feminists were demanding a counterculture space of their own.

However, where the idea of a women's company was embraced by many feminists working in alternative theatre, in the case of radical-feminist practitioners being *in the company of women* was paramount. This was especially true of the lesbian theatre scene where a pro-woman, separatist stance was important to the affirmation and celebration of lesbian women's lives and culture. Such affirmation also frequently involved directing attention to a damaging, violent system of patriarchalism. Hence, these two sides of the radical-feminist coin—valuing women's lives and experiences, and objecting to patriarchal, heterosexist structures of power and domination—circulated widely in the work of separatist companies (Freeman 1997). Equally, these dual concerns shaped plays by the foremost radical-feminist playwright, Sarah Daniels, who crafted her stories in which individual women overcome differences of class and sexuality through their shared experience of and struggle against patriarchy.

In Chapter 3, I reconnect to radical feminism through the #Me Too movement and its widely (globally) chorused demand to end a patriarchal culture that sanctions the male abuse of power (see also Part II of this introduction). Thereafter, turning to David Greig's version and revival of Aeschylus' *The Suppliant Women* (2016) and its chorus of female suppliants objecting to male control and sexual violation, I explore how the production history of this performance intersected with #Me Too, thereby amplifying radical-feminist voicings in the show and its reception. On the one hand, I address the complications and limitations of reviving the classics that arise for the 'feminist spectator as critic'; on the other, I consider how this revival elicited understandings of patriarchal power, past and present, in ways beneficial to the radical-feminist project of deconstructing and transforming it. Remaining in the realm of classical stages and restagings, Morgan Lloyd Malcolm's *Emilia* (2017) provides a companion case study: a radical-feminist treatment of the life and Shakespearean times of the poet Emilia Bassano (1569–1645). Written post-Weinstein for the Globe Theatre, *Emilia* remobilises both sides of the radical-feminist coin: stages an anger-fuelled protest at the masculinist abuse and control of women's lives and creativity, and celebrates the power of a diverse body of women acting together in the interests of other women, not only in respect of the play's subject matter but also in terms of the ensemble playing and all-female cast of players and creatives.

The democratisation of the stage evinced by the production of *Emilia* echoes the countercultural, collective feminist tradition, a tradition that was significantly eroded by the early nineties: the draconian cuts to state subsidy for the arts during the Thatcherite eighties made it difficult for an alternative theatre scene to survive.[4] As the number of feminist groups dwindled, in the main it was left to women playwrights to pass on the feminist-theatre baton. Thus, feminist energies did not vanish with the significant diminution of collectives, though they were minoritised by the male-dominated wave of in-yer-face theatre, making the nineties a relatively hard decade for women playwrights compared to their male counterparts (Aston 2003). Equally, women dramatists had to contend with the disarticulation of feminism by its reactionary, girl power double, a phenomenon that saw a redoubling of efforts on the part of feminist playwrights such as Rebecca Prichard and Judy Upton to portray the dystopian social realities for future generations of economically and socially disenfranchised young women.

Going into the twenty-first century, spearheaded by Churchill's enduring critiques of capitalism and newcomer debbie tucker green's angry, black voicings of white Western privilege, women playwrights from different generations remained in opposition to the neoliberal hegemony. During the last ten years or so, more women playwrights broke through the glass ceiling, among them: Bola Agbaje, Ella Hickson, Lucy Kirkwood, Lucy Prebble, Penelope Skinner, Nina Raine, Anya Reiss, Katherine Soper, Polly Stenham and Laura Wade. Not all of them identify with feminism and/or the left (Auld 2012), but a majority have contributed plays that swell opposition to the economic inequalities and social injustices produced by neoliberalism. Elsewhere I have offered an indicative 'feminist-theatre listing' of performances that attest to ways in which feminism on the British stage is once more set to 'enter stage left', exemplified by: works that reprise a critique of the top-girl ethos; or pay attention to economic maldistribution and exploitation; or protest at the diminution of social welfare (Aston 2018: 301–302).

Re-entering stage left, feminism has significantly expanded its critical and theoretical roots grounded in Marxist-informed class and gender analysis. Re-routing my reflections on socialist feminism via attentions to the antagonisms between the left and feminism as feminists in the seventies sought to align nascent class-gender thinking with their socialist affiliations, I arrive at the case study of *We Are the Lions Mr Manager* (2017). This touring show by Townsend Theatre recycles the popular-political, seventies theatre tradition as it restages the historic, two-year strike (August 1976–July 1978) by Asian women workers at the Grunwick film-processing laboratory. To remember Grunwick is to recollect that this took place at the time when the political pendulum swung dramatically to the right and produced the crisis on the left. Thus, my approach to *We Are the Lions Mr Manager*, with its popular-political demonstrations of how the left and feminism managed to *overcome* antagonisms in the interests of the women's strike, is to enquire after the insights this performance yields for today's ailing neoliberalism and the oppositional struggles and desires to see a swing to the *left*.

Any consideration of socialist feminism and theatre would be incomplete if it did not include Churchill, the playwright whose enduring political commitment to left-feminism on the British stage was instrumental in pioneering and developing a body of feminist-theatre criticism and theory. In my final case study, citing *Top Girls* as the play in which Churchill expressed her fears about feminism disarticulated from socialism, I come to focus on *Escaped Alone* (2016) and the reprise of her long-standing concern with the capitalist commodification and exploitation of lives and nature that render a dark, dystopian, apocalyptic future. Elucidating her political outlook as a triangulation of socialism, feminism and environmentalism, I lay claim to Churchill's theatre as an impassioned plea to address and redress the economic, social and ecological damage that capitalism produces.

To describe her eco-socialist-feminist theatre as *impassioned* is to attest to the importance of affect in shaping modes of engagement through which spectators might feel-see their way to identifying with the social and ecological values Churchill espouses. As Chantal Mouffe argues: 'The fostering of a collective will aiming at the radicalization of democracy requires mobilizing affective energy through inscription in discursive practices that beget identification with a democratic egalitarian vision' (2018: 73). That 'artistic practices' can have a 'decisive role' in the 'radicalization of democracy', Mouffe argues, 'is because, in using resources that induce emotional responses, they are able to reach human beings at the affective level' (ibid.: 77). Affect was not in the critical 'tool box' during the first wave of feminism and theatre theorising, but it has come increasingly to the fore in a raft of disciplinary contexts and is now seminal to feminist approaches to theatre, performance and neoliberalism (Diamond et al. 2017). *Restaging Feminisms* is no exception to the affective turn: methodologically, all the case studies involve critical attentions to the affective energies generated by the performances and their capacity to stimulate identifications with feminist dynamics and strategies committed to the project of recovering and radicalising democracy.

My own affective responses to the shows are threaded through performance analysis that often moves into the present tense as an attempt to enliven or reanimate the affective-political staging of feminist concerns or claims. Analysis also is interwoven with a selection of feminist literatures that serve as critical touchstones. In Chapter 2, Wade's *Home I'm Darling* is presented in dialogue with Betty Friedan's *The Feminine Mystique* (2010 [1963]); Helena Kennedy's *Eve Was Shamed* (2018) appears in conversation with Raine's *Consent*. Mary Beard's manifesto *Women and Power* (2017) cues discussion of the classical stage and centuries-long patriarchalism in Chapter 3; Campbell's *End of Equality* (2013) headlines the socialist, feminist and ecological terrain in Chapter 4, where the recirculation of Amrit Wilson's *Finding a Voice* (2018 [1978]) and Sheila Rowbotham's *Promise of A Dream* (2019 [2000]) is interwoven in the case studies (Wilson in the context of Asian women and the Grunwick strike; Rowbotham in the sixties 'promise' of social and sexual revolution).

In this introductory chapter, my citation of Mouffe, Hall and McRobbie, all of whom adopt Gramscian-informed frameworks to envision strategies for the left (left-feminism in the case of McRobbie), also signals my own critical investment in this approach. Throughout this study, I advocate the idea of feminism as a counter-hegemonic project whose struggles against neopatriarchal neoliberalism must be fought on many fronts. Equally and more specifically, by studying a range of performances staged in different kinds of venues I endorse Mouffe's notion that there are many 'possible forms of *critical* art' (2013: 91; original emphasis) that when '[e]nvisaged as counter-hegemonic interventions' can be analysed for their contribution 'to the creation of a multiplicity of sites where the dominant hegemony can be questioned' (ibid.: 104). As I have argued elsewhere, this means conceiving of 'theatre's heterogeneously formed sites of opposition to neoliberalism as a "network of resistance"', where 'critical' performances form 'links in a chain agitating for change to the neoliberal hegemony' (Aston 2016: 8).

The 'chain of equivalence among the manifold struggles against subordination' that Mouffe and Ernesto Laclau conceived to express the need for social movements to intersect (Mouffe 2018: 6), is of conceptual and structural relevance to the organisation of *Restaging Feminisms.* The chapter-by-chapter approach to each of the three feminisms and their restaging is one through which I hope the feminisms can be seen as connecting links in feminism's 'chain of equivalence' that evidences the multiple fronts on which it is resisting 'subordination': objections to feminism's neoliberal double and persistent inequalities in the legal system (Chapter 2); the struggles against a sexist patriarchal culture (Chapter 3); the fight to democratise the workplace and to end the capitalist production of ecological damage (Chapter 4).

Moreover, as an industry British theatre is not exempt from the production of inequalities; the resurgence of feminism as a social movement has seen the renewal of feminist demands to reform the inequities the industry has continued to perpetuate. Hence, what follows in Part II of this introductory chapter is an elucidation of the chain of equivalent struggles forged by: the liberal-feminist demand for parity in the industry; radical-feminist resistance to harassment in the profession; and the contestation of class and intersectional inequalities.

Part II: Equality and Diversity Matters in the British Theatre Industry

'Mind the Gender Gap'

Going into the eighties, Wandor observed that '[a] theatre industry in which the male-female ratios are equal is unlikely for some time to come' (1981: 87). For theatre to become a level-playing field, she argued the need to 'undermine' the 'male dominance' of the industry's 'workforce' and of dramatic 'subject matter'—a seismic shift that she speculated would need a policy of 'affirmative action' (ibid.).

Close on 40 years later and any statistically significant closing of the gender gap has yet to happen. Gender data sets compiled about the industry show male dominance as marginally dented rather than radically 'undermined'. Since 2012, although women playwrights and directors have seen small (single figure) percentage gains, this is nowhere near enough to redress the gender imbalance. To read that the 'proportion of plays with men at the helm has decreased from 66% in 2012 to 61% by 2014', or that plays by women had risen from 25% in 2012 to 32% in 2015 (Snow 2015), is at best a sign of incredibly slow equality progress. It is also the case that statistics can be misleading when other factors are not taken into consideration. As Joe Shellard reports in 'Mind the Gender Gap' (2016), any measure of women's playwriting 'success' needs to be qualified by data that also evidences if their work appeared on a main stage or in a studio space; whether their plays had long or short runs compared to male playwrights; and a gender-breakdown of ticket prices and revenue. Moreover, the reality of the gender gap can also be obscured by commentaries in the press vaunting the idea that 'for the first time in history' young women playwrights 'have the theatrical establishment at their feet' (Auld 2012). In other words, it would be more accurate to applaud a young generation of women writers gaining a firm foothold in an industry still riddled with male-dominated gatekeeping. Frustrated by the lack of progress, commentators such as activist and blogger Victoria Sadler, who provides an annual review of the numbers of plays by women in London's major, subsidised theatres, put this more starkly: 'At what point are we going to stop excusing difficulties around attaining gender parity and state clearly that there is discrimination against women writers in theatre?' (Sadler 2018).

Although important to track discrimination and inequality in the industry, problematically the action of reporting does not in and of itself automatically lead to change. Sue Parrish, Artistic Director of Sphinx Theatre (formerly The Women's Theatre Group), who has campaigned untiringly for equality, observes that she has 'a stack of exhaustive and comprehensive reports of women's representation on stage and backstage since the one [she] commissioned in 1983 for the Conference of Women Theatre Directors and Administrators' (2018). 'At its publication', she explains, 'we naively assumed that once the data was known justice would quickly follow' (ibid.). Why the continued injustice, 'why the inevitable progress women in the industry had been envisaging since the 1970s still hadn't materialised' (Kerbel 2017: 7) and the all-important question of how to tackle it, are matters that have come to the fore in the present climate of renewed feminist objections to persistent inequalities.

A key obstacle in the subsidised sector to gender parity is the historic and continued deployment of a funding model that favours male leadership with a larger slice of the financial cake. Statistics for 2014 regarding artistic directors in the National Portfolio Organisations (NPOs) funded by Arts Council England (ACE) evidence that in organisations in receipt of £500,000 or above, 76% (35) of directors are male; in organisations below the £500,000 threshold, 59% (84) are male. The overall gender imbalance is 63% (119) of male directors, compared to 37% (69) female.[5] With a funding model that grants significantly more power to men than women at senior levels, it becomes clear that, as Wandor advised, the status quo will not shift without proactive actions.

Hence, campaigns and calls for liberal-feminist or equality-feminist reforms have gathered momentum, notably the call to introduce quota systems. ERA 50:50 (Equal Representation for Actresses) campaign founded in 2015 by actresses Lizzie Berrington and Polly Kemp is fighting for 50:50 gender quotas across the theatre, film and television industries to be achieved by 2020. The Act for Change Project launched in 2014 campaigns and lobbies for an end to discrimination and promotion of equality and diversity in the arts, and several, major theatres in receipt of ACE funding have pledged to adopt equality-related strategies. Some of them have been advised and assisted by Tonic Theatre, an organisation founded by Lucy Kerbel in 2011 to support the industry in taking steps towards equality, often by making small, incremental changes to policies and working practices that 'combine to produce a bigger effect' (Kerbel 2017: 20). Building on 'the tireless campaigning conducted by individual women and women's theatre groups over the last few decades' (ibid.: 37), Kerbel deliberately chose to work with high-profile theatres in receipt of major funding, 'because we knew that if they changed how they made work, took decisions, and built their artistic programme, they would take others with them' (ibid.: 8). Theatres that have worked with Tonic include the National Theatre where Artistic Director Rufus Norris has committed to achieving a 50:50 gender split for women directors and playwrights by 2021 (see Chapter 2)[6]—a notably different stance to his predecessor Nicholas Hytner. In his term of office at the National (2003–2015), Hytner never directed a play by a woman writer (Pascal 2018); at the helm of the new, commercial Bridge Theatre, which opened in 2017, he refuses to countenance quotas.

For their part, ACE did endorse a commitment to equality and diversity by stipulating that for its 2018–2022 grant cycle NPOs had to include an equality action plan as part of their funding bid. The Council's guide to writing a SMART action plan (ACE 2017) reminds NPOs of the need to comply with the Equality Act (2010), referencing the nine protected characteristics covered by this legislation.[7] As a future-orientated document it has far less to say about the Council's historic failings: the introduction by the then CEO Darren Henley refers repeatedly to what the organisation wants to achieve, rather than admitting to or taking responsibility for the inequalities it has perpetuated. Arriving late at the equality and diversity table, what the Arts Council wants to see is the adoption of an inclusive approach to the work that it funds. While this appears to be a step in the right direction, it remains to be seen whether this is merely an image-making exercise. As Sara Ahmed cautions, statements on behalf of organisations that express a commitment to equality and diversity often constitute 'non-performative' speech acts—'non-performative' because they act 'as if they bring about what they name' (2005: §3). Following Ahmed, there are serious questions to be asked and reservations to be had about whether the Council's statement and the equality reports it now demands from NPOs will prove 'non-performative': the *act* of reporting on equality matters substituting for the doing of equality *actions*.

With respect to gender parity, a genuine commitment on the part of NPOs to 'act for change' could make a significant difference to theatre's malestream: pave the way for women-centred narratives to move centre stage in more equal numbers. Indeed, more roles for women are essential to levelling the 2:1, male to female, ratio of performers. However, it is not just a question of creating more roles for women, but of considering what kinds of roles and whether these are central, rather than marginal, to the action, and so forth. One litmus test aimed specifically at the dominance of male-centred narratives is the Bechdel-inspired Sphinx Test, devised and developed by Parrish's company after wide consultation with writers and directors. The test prompts theatre makers to consider whether there is a woman centre stage, whether she is a complex character actively driving the dramatic action in a culturally impactful drama. One way to think of the test is as a consciousness-raising exercise that if widely adopted by theatre companies and venues, could help stimulate writing (by women and men) that does not cast women to the margins of the stage action and narrative. Equally, as a consciousness-raising device its usage can extend to interrogating the category of 'woman' through a diversity lens, thereby raising crucial questions such as: Is there a woman of colour centre stage?[8]

Ultimately, irrespective of what, if any, strategies are adopted, from quotas through incremental shifts in policies and practices, to the writing of more complex and diversity-aware roles for women performers, change is neither achievable nor sustainable if equality matters to theatres only as an issue of duty and legal compliance. As theatre critic Lyn Gardner put it: 'It's not just about the numbers, it's about the whole culture of an organisation' (2017). In short, as Chapter 2 will detail, it is at the limit of what equality-led, feminist strategies can achieve that the need to intersect with other feminisms can be felt. Keeping that in mind, a next step to consider is that any reform of the British theatre industry must necessarily include transforming the patriarchal culture of the profession—the kind of transformation that traditionally has characterised the terrain of radical feminism.

From Inappropriate Behaviour to a Code of Behaviour

In her discussion of equality, diversity and non-performative speech acts, Ahmed offers the image of the apple that looks 'big shiny red' on the outside, but 'rotten' at the 'core' (2005: §33). The rottenness at the core of the UK's entertainment industry became visible in 2012 when, in the year after the death of television entertainer Jimmy Savile, revelations were made about his historic and systematic abuse of women and children. To present another image: like a stone thrown into water, the ripple effect of this case swelled to include more and more cases in the industry and in other public institutions. As Helena Kennedy QC explains, this generated public debate on an unprecedented scale: 'How could so many predators have got away with it? Why did people do nothing?' (2018: 4). 'Patriarchy', the 'virus that lives deep in the body politic' needed, she claimed, to be named and changed (ibid.: 9).

The naming and shaming of patriarchy went viral in October 2017 through #Me Too, the social-media campaign ignited by the sexual-abuse allegations made by female stars against Hollywood film producer, Harvey Weinstein. The hashtag functioned like a distress signal in Morse code: women, not just movie celebrities, but women from all walks of life across the globe, tapping out their declarations that sexual harassment, or other forms of male violence, had happened to 'me too'. This radical-feminist outcry against harassment and proclamation of anti-patriarchal solidarity (see Chapter 3), attested to the patriarchal 'virus' as a deadly disease of pandemic proportions.

With the UK's entertainment industry already reeling from the fallout from the Savile case, the domino-effect of #Me Too saw British theatre taking stock of sexual harassment in the ranks of its profession. Two cases received widespread media attention. One involved London's Old Vic Theatre: having honoured its outgoing Artistic Director, Kevin Spacey, at the Olivier Awards in 2015, in the autumn of 2017 the Old Vic stood accused of covering up Spacey's inappropriate sexual behaviour—in this case, chiefly towards young men. It was the #Me Too movement that inspired actor Anthony Rapp to speak out about an instance of alleged sexual abuse by Spacey that dated back to the eighties when Rapp would have been just fourteen years old.[9] This encouraged others to come forward, with further allegations testifying to the Old Vic's lack of a clear grievance procedure and confidence that complaints would be heard and taken seriously given Spacey's star status.

A second fallen idol was Max Stafford-Clark, former Artistic Director of the Royal Court Theatre, founder of Joint Stock and subsequently the Out of Joint theatre company. In September 2017, Stafford-Clark was forced to resign from Out of Joint after a formal complaint of harassment was made by Gina Abolins from the company's theatre-education wing. No public statement was made about the complaint; thus, while the company had listened and acted, it had also covered up the director's alleged inappropriate behaviour. However, in the wake of the Weinstein scandal, a report by Alexandra Topping for the *Guardian* ousted Abolins' complaint and cited more women claiming they were subjected to verbal, sexual abuse by the director (2017). Topping's story broke on Friday 20th October; by Monday 23rd October, the *Guardian* was reporting on a statement signed by leading figures in British theatres, condemning sexual harassment and committing to 'working together to ensure that theatre is a safe space for all, where everyone is respected and listened to' (Grierson 2017).

One of the signatories to that letter was Vicky Featherstone, Artistic Director of the Royal Court (2013–). As testimony to Featherstone's performative rather than non-performative intentions, she announced a day of action to be hosted at the Court on Saturday 28th October: 'No Grey Area'. The event included a public reading of 150 testimonies in the theatre's main auditorium and a series of town hall meetings convened in its studio space. The aim was not to name and shame, but to hear evidences of how theatre practitioners had been affected by abuses of power and, through a process of sharing and listening, to draw up a Code of Behaviour for the theatre industry. What the Code of Behaviour advocates is: taking responsibility for power; having reporting structures in place; raising awareness of all staff through a code of practice; and recognising the broad scope of the industry, its range of creative practices and contexts, thereby identifying areas of work where staff may be particularly at risk. As a document, its strength lies in its rejection of the finely crafted, potentially non-performative policy statement. Rather, as an immediate response, it constitutes 'an offering, a provocation, a hope for culture change'.[10]

Historically, as Beard's manifesto on *Women and Power* (2017) attests, the silencing of women's voices in the public sphere is a centuries-old phenomenon. And when the voicings of radical-feminist sensibilities reverberate against the walls of patriarchy, they are more likely than not to be ridiculed or subjected to backlash manoeuvres, as evidenced in the case of the #Me Too backlash (see Chapter 3). However, one cautiously optimistic sign is that Featherstone's feminist voice and those of other theatre makers demanding change, are being listened to within and beyond the sector: in the 2018 'Stage 100 List' of the most influential figures in the theatre industry, Featherstone was ranked first because of the stance she took on sexual harassment. Thus, influential women *and* men working *inside* the structures of power can help to bring about and shape a culture change, but only if they exercise a different system of power to that of the masculinist model. As the draft Code of Behaviour advocates, this means power to be exercised responsibly in non-exploitative ways.

Class Acts and Intersectional Inequalities

Equality-focused strategies and the radical-feminist demand to end the abuse of male power are two important links in this chain of equivalent struggles to resist and transform subordination within the theatre system. A third link concerns the material conditions for those women *and* men in the lower echelons of the industry.

The economic precarity of many workers in the profession is not a new circumstance, but it is a worsening condition in which social and economic capital is militating against equal opportunities. British theatre's class ceiling increasingly restricts opportunities for working-class performers to enter and advance in the profession. In this regard, economic capital, or rather lack thereof, is a significant gatekeeper. The costs of entering the profession (auditions for drama school and the finances needed to support a conservatoire education) are prohibitive for those from low economic backgrounds. Equally, economic precarity haunts those lucky enough to climb the first rungs of the industry's ladder; many are forced to take unpaid or low-paid positions and live with the uncertainty of freelancing from one project to the next. In short, barriers to social mobility within the arts have strengthened rather than weakened, rendering the acting profession a club for the wealthy elite. Thus, among leading, working-class actors from older generations there is a widely shared view that this 'new economic shift [...] excludes many would-be actors from breaking into the profession' (Thorpe 2016). Equally, the view that class is a significant barrier to participation in the arts is substantiated by a raft of surveys, notably the 2015 'Panic!' report, a national survey for the UK's creative and cultural industries.[11]

Unlike gender which is a protected characteristic, there is no protection against social class discrimination.[12] Hence, discriminatory practices perpetuated by the middle-class bias of the profession go unchecked. For instance, the chances of a young, working-class woman from the North succeeding at an audition for one of the London drama schools are radically reduced when it is her Northern accent that is used to classify her as working class: not 'posh' enough for the middle-class milieu of the conservatoire and acting profession that privileges received pronunciation. Stereotyping of the Northern 'character' plays a detrimental part too; as leading actress Maxine Peake attests: 'There is only one class in the north, and that's working class, and if you're a woman you will be slightly brassy and a bit blowzy; if you're a man you're either aggressive or you're angsty and poetic. That is the entire north in a nutshell' (qtd. in Brown 2018).

At the time of second-wave feminism, the recognition that class acts as a barrier to social mobility was foundational to socialist feminists who posited the class struggle as the basis for a *common* struggle with men. The articulation of a class struggle in contemporary British theatre, if I might be permitted to name it as such, augers class as the basis on which those women and men who identify or are identified as working class might find common ground in the fight to change an industry riven by class discrimination. Already there are fledging initiatives underway to support and promote working-class diversity, including the Arts

Emergency mentorship scheme and Common Theatre set up by David Loumgair to mirror the gender-focused enterprise of organisations such as Tonic Theatre.

The class struggle in British theatre also relates to the relative decline in plays and performances representing working-class lives and experiences—especially those of working-class women. Crediting Shelagh Delaney and her iconoclastic *Taste of Honey* (1958) 'in paving the way for a subsequent generation of working-class playwrights (mostly men)', Gardner finds it 'astonishing' that 'British theatre is still tying itself up in knots over the lack of working-class representation: on its stages, in its workforce, and in its audience' (2019). Contemporary Delaneys are hard to find; the class struggle prohibits the possibility that 'a 19-year-old Shelagh Delaney living in Salford today [would] have the interest in and access to theatre as her namesake 60 years ago, or the confidence to write her own play' (ibid.). Hence, nothing short of a class-gender-power-quake is needed to redress the 60-year trend in which working-class women's stories have been largely absent from the British stage.[13] As working-class actress Julie Hesmondhalgh speculates about television and related arts industries: 'If people from working-class backgrounds were in decision-making positions and working as directors and writers [...] then that would make space for more complex portrayals of life in more marginalized parts of society' (2019: 155).

It is not only class that creates an additional equality barrier for women in theatre; other supposedly protected characteristics also combine with gender to produce inequalities. For decades, women in the industry have complained about the dearth of roles for older actresses, which is why Churchill's *Escaped Alone* with its cast of four elder women is so exceptional (see Chapter 4). At the intersection of gender, age and race, roles are even harder to find, as black, British actress Natasha Gordon attests, describing how she 'was always the support: the friend, the nurse or the teacher. I never got the opportunity to discover what it was like to lead a company' (qtd. in Crompton 2018). Her experience is borne out by research which shows that BAME women routinely face the problem of being offered roles that they are 'uncomfortable with', either because they conform to racialised stereotyping, or because parts do not speak 'to the BAME, female and working class experience in Britain that [goes] beyond what [is] perceived to be a white, middle class, cultural establishment's view of their lives' (O'Brien 2015).

In Gordon's case, the frustration over the lack or type of roles available saw her scripting a debut drama. *Nine Night*, based on the Jamaican ritual of mourning and celebrating the death of a loved one, was staged at the National Theatre (2018), a sold-out run that earned her a transfer to the Trafalgar Studios, the Charles Winter Award for Most Promising Playwright and the accolade of being the first black British woman playwright to be produced in the West End. But she is ambiguous about this success: 'How can I celebrate that in 2018? If I want to take that as an individual achievement, then sure, but what does that do towards moving us forward and opening the ground for the younger generation' (qtd. in Minamore 2018). Gordon's concern about 'opening the ground for the younger generation' is widely shared by BAME women in the industry, as reflected in Stella Kanu's initiative at the Ovalhouse in 2018: #Connect: Black Women in Theatre.[14] Conceived as an informal gathering to host inter-generational conversations, the demand for this event was such that it has grown into a series of regularly convened meetings, celebrated on 25 July 2019 with a photograph imaging 250 black women theatre makers on the Globe's stage. Tagged 'WeAreVisible' and using the occasion to formally name the connect events as Black Womxn in Theatre (womxn signifying inclusivity, the recognition of non-binary and trans women), the photo shoot renders a joyous, collectivist picture of black womxn's achievements. However, despite how the reincarnated Globe eschews the Elizabethan all-male tradition (see Chapter 3), as the backdrop to the photograph, Shakespeare's theatre is a salutary reminder of the white, male privilege and cultural gatekeeping that endure as impediments to the inclusivity that the black womxn theatre makers aspire to. Thus, as the image records black womxn's accomplishments, it also gestures to the ongoing struggles to achieve cultural diversity on the British stage.

In sum: on the one hand, when viewed by the feminist who takes stock of equality matters, who sees the gender trouble caused by a prevalent culture of sexual harassment and recognises class and intersectional inequalities, the picture that emerges of British theatre is far from the equality- and diversity-welcoming body that ACE claims it would like it to be. On the other, she can also see how the democratic demands to 'act for change' have gained traction, thereby building on and renewing the claims to equality that second-wave feminists set in motion. And it is in the context and spirit of agitating for change in British theatre that I set my trio of 'restaging feminisms' chapters in motion, turning first to the 'drama' of liberal feminism.

Notes

1. The public artwork was designed and curated by Artichoke run by Helen Marriage and Nicky Webb.
2. This notably arose in the wake of Judith Butler's anti-essentialist theorisation of gender when it became difficult to opt for a position that appeared essentialist.
3. For details of these companies and others on the alternative theatre scene, see the 'Unfinished Histories' website: https://www.unfinishedhistories.com/.
4. The two notable exceptions are Clean Break and The Women's Theatre Group, renamed as Sphinx Theatre Company.
5. Statistics recorded on Tonic Theatre's website: http://www.tonictheatre-advance.co.uk/advance-2014/learning/#stats.
6. The National Theatre also worked with the Act for Change Project.
7. The nine protected characteristics are: age, disability, gender/sex, gender re-assignment, marriage and civil partnership, pregnancy and maternity, race, religion/belief, sexual orientation.
8. Although the Sphinx Test was designed with theatre makers in mind, I have found it a valuable springboard for discussion in the context of teaching feminism and theatre, and I recommend it as such.
9. Spacey invoked the ire of the LGBTQ community by coupling his initial response to Rapp's allegation with coming out as a gay man, thus conflating his predation of a male minor with his claim to a gay identity.
10. The Code of Behaviour can be accessed on the Royal Court's website: https://royalcourttheatre.com/code-of-behaviour/. Other theatres picked up the code-of-behaviour baton; several, including the National, reviewed their extant policies and/or established other industry-wide initiatives. The Old Vic's remedial action has been to introduce a 'Guardians Programme' for the arts and other sectors.
11. The findings of this survey 'provide hard evidence for the common impression that the arts sector is a closed shop where most people are middle class' http://www.createlondon.org/panic/survey/. Among a raft of telling statistics, it reveals that 76% of respondents 'had at least one parent working in a managerial or professional (i.e. "middle class") job whilst they were growing up and that over half had at least one parent with a degree whilst growing up' (ibid.). See also the follow-up project 'Panic!2018': https://createlondon.org/event/panic2018/ and the Labour Party's commissioned 'inquiry into access and diversity in the performing arts': 'Acting Up Report' (2017).
12. In the Council's 'Guide to Producing Equality Action Plans and Objectives for NPOs', class appears as a supplementary note under an

explanatory paragraph on diversity: 'We also include class and economic disadvantage and social and institutional barriers that prevent people from participating in and enjoying the arts' (ACE 2017).

13. In December 2017, not long after hosting the 'No Grey Area' day of action, Featherstone courted controversy when she made the difficult decision to withdraw a scheduled revival of *Rita Sue and Bob Too* by the working-class playwright, Andrea Dunbar (1961–1990). Originally directed by Stafford-Clark when it was staged at the Court in 1982 and revived by his Out of Joint company in 2017, Featherstone felt conflicted: the play's subject matter—two teen girls used and groomed by a man for his sexual pleasure—appeared to contradict the stance she had taken over sexual harassment and was haunted by the hand of the disgraced director. She decided to cancel the production, but reversed her decision following accusations of censorship aired in the press. The censoring of a playwright's voice went against the Court's reputation as a writers' theatre, and it would have meant absenting the voice of one of the few working-class, women playwrights to be heard on the Court's stage.
14. In 2018, Kanu was Executive Producer of the Ovalhouse in Kennington, London, tasked with overseeing the venue's relocation to a new, purpose-built theatre in Brixton, scheduled for completion in 2020. Between 2018 and 2019, the Ovalhouse hosted three #Connect: Black Women in Theatre events. Given Kanu's move to Executive Director of the London International Festival of Theatre and the relocation of the Oval, the intention is to seek a new venue to host the meetings.

Works Cited

Ahmed, S. 2005. The Non-Performativity of Anti-Racism. *Borderlands* (e-journal) 5 (3).

Armstrong, S. 2017. *The New Poverty*. London: Verso.

Arruza, C., T. Bhattacharya, and N. Fraser. 2019. *Feminism for the 99%: A Manifesto*. London: Verso.

Arts Council England. 2017. Guide to Producing Equality Action Plans and Objectives for NPOs. https://www.artscouncil.org.uk/sites/default/files/download-file/Equality%20Action%20Guide%20-%20Introduction.pdf.

Aston, E. 2003. *Feminist Views on the English Stage: Women Playwrights, 1990–2000*. Cambridge: Cambridge University Press.

———. 2016. Agitating for Change: Theatre and a Feminist 'Network of Resistance'. *Theatre Research International* 41 (1): 5–20.

———. 2018. Enter Stage Left: 'Recognition', 'Redistribution', and the A-Affect. *Contemporary Theatre Review* 28 (3): 299–309.

Auld, T. 2012. Angry Young Women: The New Generation of Young Female Playwrights. *Daily Telegraph*, 8 May. https://www.telegraph.co.uk/culture/theatre/theatre-features/9239192/Angry-young-women-the-new-generation-of-young-female-playwrights.html.

Beard, M. 2017. *Women and Power: A Manifesto*. London: Profile Books.

Brown, M. 2018. Arts Industry Report Asks: Where Are All the Working-Class People? *Guardian*, 16 April. https://www.theguardian.com/culture/2018/apr/16/arts-industry-report-asks-where-are-all-the-working-class-people.

Cameron, D. 2010. Big Society Speech. Gov.UK, 19 July. https://www.gov.uk/government/speeches/big-society-speech.

Campbell, B. 2013. *End of Equality: The Only Way Is Women's Liberation*. London: Seagull.

Case, S. 2008 [1988]. *Feminism and Theatre*. Basingstoke: Palgrave Macmillan.

Cochrane, K. 2013. The Fourth Wave of Feminism: Meet the Rebel Women. *Guardian*, 10 December. https://www.theguardian.com/world/2013/dec/10/fourth-wave-feminism-rebel-women.

Crenshaw, K. 1989. Demarginalizing the Intersection of Race and Sex: A Black Feminist Critique of Antidiscrimination Doctrine, Feminist Theory and Antiracist Politics. *University of Chicago Legal Forum*, 1 (8): 139–167.

Crompton, S. 2018. Natasha Gordon Interview. *Independent*, 30 November. https://www.independent.co.uk/arts-entertainment/theatre-dance/features/natasha-gordon-interview-nine-night-trafalgar-studios-play-a8659091.html.

Davis, K. 2008. Intersectionality as Buzzword: A Sociology of Science Perspective on What Makes a Feminist Theory Successful. *Feminist Theory* 9 (1): 67–85.

Diamond, E., D. Varney, and C. Amich. 2017. *Performance, Feminism and Affect in Neoliberal Times*. London: Palgrave Macmillan.

Dolan, J. 2012 [1988]. *The Feminist Spectator as Critic*. Ann Arbor: University of Michigan Press.

Eddo-Lodge, R. 2018 [2017]. *Why I'm No Longer Talking to White People About Race*. London: Bloomsbury.

Evans, E. 2015. *The Politics of Third Wave Feminisms: Neoliberalism, Intersectionality, and the State in Britain and the US*. Basingstoke: Palgrave Macmillan.

Freeman, S. 1997. *Putting Your Daughters on the Stage: Lesbian Theatre from the 1970s to the 1990s*. London: Cassell.

Friedan, B. 2010 [1963]. *The Feminine Mystique*. London: Penguin.

Gardner, L. 2017. It's Time the UK's Top Theatre Committed to Gender Quotas. *The Stage*, 18 September. https://www.thestage.co.uk/opinion/2017/lyn-gardner-time-uks-top-theatres-committed-gender-quotas/.

———. 2019. Theatre's Class Ceiling. Digital Theatre+, 29 March. https://www.digitaltheatreplus.com/education/news/lyn-gardner-on-theatre-and-performance-theatres-class-ceiling.

Grierson, J. 2017. British Theatre Bosses Condemn Sexual Harassment in the Industry. *Guardian*, 23 October. https://www.theguardian.com/stage/2017/oct/23/british-theatre-bosses-condemn-sexual-harassment-in-industry.

Hall, S. 1988. *The Hard Road to Renewal: Thatcherism and the Crisis of the Left*. London: Verso.

Hemmings, C. 2011. *Why Stories Matter: The Political Grammar of Feminist Theory*. Durham: Duke University.

Hesford, V. 2013. *Feeling Women's Liberation*. Durham: Duke University.

Hesmondhalgh, J. 2019. *Julie Hesmondhalgh: A Working Diary*. London: Bloomsbury.

Heywood, L., and J. Drake. 1997. *Third Wave Agenda: Being Feminist, Doing Feminism*. Minneapolis: University of Minnesota Press.

Jones, O. 2011. *Chavs: The Demonization of the Working Class*. London: Verso.

Kennedy, H. 2018. *Eve Was Shamed: How British Justice Is Failing Women*. London: Chatto & Windus.

Kerbel, L. 2017. *All Change Please: A Practical Guide for Achieving Gender Equality in Theatre*. London: Nick Hern.

Labour Party. 2017. Acting Up Report: Labour's Inquiry into Access and Diversity in the Performing Arts. https://d3n8a8pro7vhmx.cloudfront.net/campaigncountdown/pages/1157/attachments/original/1502725031/Acting-Up-Report.pdf?1502725031.

Lansley, S., and J. Mack. 2015. *Breadline Britain: The Rise of Mass Poverty*. London: Oneworld.

Lovenduski, J., and V. Randall. 1993. *Contemporary Feminist Politics: Women and Power in Britain*. Oxford: Oxford University Press.

Mackay, F. 2015. *Radical Feminism: Feminist Activism in Movement*. Basingstoke: Palgrave Macmillan.

McRobbie, A. 2009. *The Aftermath of Feminism: Gender, Culture and Social Change*. London: Sage.

Minamore, B. 2018. 'We're here!' The Black Playwrights Storming the West End. *Guardian*, 3 October. https://www.theguardian.com/stage/2018/oct/03/west-end-black-theatre-misty-arinze-kene-nine-night-natasha-gordon.

Mouffe, C. 2013. *Agonistics: Thinking the World Politically*. London: Verso.

———. 2018. *For a Left Populism*. London: Verso.

O'Brien, D. 2015. The Class Problem in British Acting: Talking at Camden People's Theatre. *Stratification and Culture Research Network*, 27 April. https://stratificationandculture.wordpress.com/2015/04/27/the-class-problem-in-british-acting-talking-at-camden-peoples-theatre/.

Parrish, S. 2018. We Must Break Down Barriers to Gender Parity. *The Stage*, 8 March. https://www.thestage.co.uk/opinion/2018/sphinx-theatres-sue-parrish-we-must-break-down-barriers-to-gender-parity/.

Pascal, J. 2018. Women are Being Excluded from the Stage: It's Time for Quotas. *Guardian*, 24 April. https://www.theguardian.com/commentisfree/2018/apr/24/women-theatre-quotas-stage-gender.

Rowbotham, S. 2019 [2000]. *Promise of a Dream: Remembering the Sixties.* London: Verso.

Royal Court Theatre. 2017. Code of Behaviour. https://royalcourttheatre.com/code-of-behaviour/.

Sadler, V. 2018. Theatre in Review: Challenges for Female Playwrights Continues. VictoriaSadler.com, 4 September. http://www.victoriasadler.com/2018-theatre-in-review-challenges-for-female-playwrights-continues/.

Seymour, R. 2016. *Corbyn: The Strange Rebirth of Radical Politics.* London: Verso.

Shellard, J. 2016. Mind the Gender Gap. *Purple Seven Theatre Magazine*, May, 41–42.

Snow, G. 2015. Women 'Edge Towards Equality in Theatre'. *The Stage*, 10 December. https://www.thestage.co.uk/news/2015/gender-equality-moving-in-right-direction-claims-study/.

Thorpe, V. 2016. New Study Exposes 'Class Ceiling' That Deters Less Privileged Actors. *Guardian*, 27 February. https://www.theguardian.com/culture/2016/feb/27/class-ceiling-working-class-actors-study.

Topping, A. 2017. Theatre Director Max Stafford-Clark Was Ousted over Inappropriate Behaviour. *Guardian*, 20 October. https://www.theguardian.com/stage/2017/oct/20/theatre-director-max-stafford-clark-was-ousted-over-inappropriate-behaviour.

Tyler, I. 2013. *Revolting Subjects: Social Abjection and Resistance in Neoliberal Britain*. London: Zed.

Wandor, M. 1981. *Understudies: Theatre and Sexual Politics.* London: Eyre Methuen.

———. 1986. *Carry On, Understudies: Theatre and Sexual Politics.* London: Routledge & Kegan Paul.

Weeks, K. 2014. Foreword. *Women's Oppression Today: The Marxist/Feminist Encounter*, ix–xix. M. Barrett. London: Verso.

Wilson, A. 2018 [1978]. *Finding a Voice: Asian Women in Britain*, 2nd ed., n.p. Daraja Press.

Websites

Act for Change. https://www.act-for-change.com/.

Arts Emergency. https://arts-emergency.org/.

Common Theatre. https://commontheatre.co.uk/.

ERA 50: 50. http://equalrepresentationforactresses.co.uk/.

Panic! http://www.createlondon.org/panic/.

Purple Seven. https://purplesevenanalytics.com/.
Tonic Theatre. https://www.tonictheatre.co.uk/.
Unfinished Histories. https://www.unfinishedhistories.com/.

CHAPTER 2

Reviewing the Drama of Liberal Feminism

Abstract Contextualising histories of liberalism, new liberalism, neoliberalism and feminism, the chapter offers a reassessment of liberal feminism via two case studies: Laura Wade's *Home, I'm Darling* and Nina Wade's *Consent*, two productions staged at London's National Theatre. The argument of the chapter is twofold: firstly, it contends that the unmasking of liberal feminism's neoliberal double is essential to disarticulating the idea of the self-empowered, autonomous, individual woman. Secondly, it argues that it is at the limit of what equality-focused feminism can achieve in terms of social change that connections can be made to the socially transformative ends of radical and/or socialist feminisms. Betty Friedan's liberal-feminist critique of the 'feminine mystique' is re-encountered through Wade's play; Raine's *Consent* reprises the feminist issue of equality before the law.

Keywords Liberal feminism · Choice feminism · Feminine mystique · Neoliberal mystique · Equality and the law

Have we reached the 'limits' of liberal feminism as Miranda Kiraly and Meagan Tyler suggest in the title of their Australian anthology *Freedom Fallacy: The Limits of Liberal Feminism* (2015)? Most contributors to their anthology support a 'radical challenge to the dominance of liberal-feminist discourse in the public sphere'; a few recognise that 'liberal feminism can still be seen to have made some contribution to the women's

E. Aston, *Restaging Feminisms*,
https://doi.org/10.1007/978-3-030-40589-2_2

liberation movement' (Kiraly and Tyler 2015: xvii–xviii). This assessment differs radically from Zillah R. Eisenstein's evaluation of liberal feminism in *The Radical Future of Liberal Feminism* published in 1981. Although acknowledging the limitations of liberal feminism, Eisenstein's title predicted that liberal feminism would be 'radical' in its 'future' iterations. However, this was contingent on achieving a 'heightened political understanding' of the limitations of liberal feminism: the recognition that a 'liberal state cannot meet the demands of woman's equality', thus paving the way for liberal feminists to be in dialogue with the more socially transformative aspirations of radical and socialist feminists (Eisenstein 1981: 9).

Instead of a 'heightened political understanding' of liberal feminism's limitations, what transpired over time was a neoliberal appropriation of a liberal-feminist lexis that transformed equality and rights into the 'freedom fallacy': the illusion of women's self-empowerment and choice that flies in the face of persistent inequalities and social injustices. When refracted through the lens of choice feminism, the contributions liberal feminism has made—and still might yet make—to struggles for equality are rendered null and void.

There is also more at stake here than the question mark that hangs over the future of liberal feminism. History repeatedly shows liberal feminism to be the mainstream, popular face of feminism. As Eisenstein complained: 'feminists and nonfeminists often mistakenly assume that it *is* feminism' to the detriment of feminism's heterogeneity which is 'rendered nonexistent' (1981: 4; original emphasis). When it is assumed that *neoliberal* choice feminism '*is* feminism' not only does it invalidate an equality-focused agenda since freedom is deemed to be achieved, but it is also risking the disarticulation of all socially progressive feminisms. To loosen the hegemonic hold of choice feminism over the popular imagination is therefore advantageous to all feminisms committed to recognising, addressing and transforming enduring inequalities.

My argument in this chapter is therefore twofold. On the one hand, I contend it is vital to contest the 'freedom fallacy' vaunted by neoliberal choice feminism. On the other, echoing Eisenstein, I recognise that it is at the limit of what equality-focused feminism can achieve in terms of social change that connections might be made to the socially transformative ends of radical and/or socialist feminisms. In other words, the limitations of the former demand the radicalism of the latter. The unmasking of choice feminism is a critical manoeuvre performed in the first of my two case studies: Laura Wade's *Home, I'm Darling* (2018), a satirical portrait of a middle-class housewife-by-choice who revives the 'feminine mystique' that was the object of Betty Friedan's liberal-feminist critique. Nina Raine's *Consent* (2017), my second case study, echoes liberal feminism's long-standing concern with equality before the law: puts the UK's legal system on trial for its failure to achieve justice for women in rape cases.

Home, I'm Darling and *Consent* are the first plays by Wade and Raine to be performed at London's National Theatre. *Home, I'm Darling* was a co-production with Theatr Clwyd, Wales, where the show premiered in June 2018 before arriving at the National; *Consent* was a co-production with Out of Joint which opened at the National in April 2017. Both plays transferred to the West End: *Home I'm Darling* went on to the Duke of York's Theatre; *Consent* had a run at the Harold Pinter Theatre. In 2019 *Home, I'm Darling* won the Olivier Award for Best New Comedy.

My approach to the plays involves my own feminist responses to or impressions of the shows and their impressions of feminism—notably impressions of liberal/neoliberal feminism/s. Further, I present and engage in a critical dialogue between each play and a primary text: Friedan's *The Feminine Mystique* (1963) is resurrected in the discussion of *Home, I'm Darling*; Helena Kennedy's *Eve Was Shamed* (2018) appears beside and in conversation with *Consent*. As stated in Chapter 1, I am not arguing that either play is written from a liberal-feminist perspective: Wade shows the damaging effects of liberal feminism restaged as choice feminism; Raine contests the idea that the liberal state upholds women's rights in law, at least as far as the question of consent is concerned.

Historically, the UK's liberal state never readily consented to women's rights; these had to be fought for. Before embarking on the case studies, a brief consideration of the historical 'drama' depicting the complex and contradictory relations between liberalism and liberal feminism will help to contextualise how and why a liberal-feminist discourse has been appropriated by neoliberalism (Wade) and liberal-feminist reform is not in itself enough to effect social change (Raine).

Histories of Liberalism, New Liberalism, Neoliberalism and Liberal Feminism

Philosophically, politically and historically, liberalism has championed the liberties of the individual—liberties endorsed and supported by a seemingly non-interventionist state designed to give free reign to a market economy. By the nineteenth century, liberalism had become hegemonic in the sense that liberal ideas, politics and practices dominated and shaped British governmentality, economic, civil and intellectual life. Contrastingly, by the close of the nineteenth century that hegemony was under threat. In their Gramscian-based analysis of the 'crisis of liberalism' between 1880 and 1930, Stuart Hall and Bill Schwarz explain that ruptures in hegemonic formations occur when 'the social formation can no longer be reproduced on the basis of pre-existing social relations' (Hall and Schwarz 1988: 95, 96). The 'pre-existing social relations' of the liberal state did not entertain the idea of women's (or indeed universal) suffrage: class, property and gender determined the limits of enfranchisement. Thus, while women's demand for the constitutional right to vote was in one way a liberal demand for political representation through which they might enhance their opportunities and individual liberties, in another it was also oppositional to the liberal system that denied their citizenry. That opposition was cast 'in most dramatic terms' through the militant actions of the suffragettes, rendered visible and palpable in the moment

> when male political leaders looked out from the Palace of Westminster to see their female relatives and social acquaintances breaking through the police cordons in order to reach the parliament building and demonstrate their passionate and public condemnation of that exclusively masculine bastion of political power. (ibid.: 103)

Conjuring up that historic moment of suffragette militancy, Hall and Schwarz foreground the affective ('passionate') charge against liberal governance and the limitations of a liberalism enmeshed in patriarchalism ('masculine bastion of political power').

Furthermore, liberalism's creed of individualism was opposed by factions ideologically committed to the idea of collectivism. Such factions ranged across the political spectrum from the extreme right with its view of 'imperialist collectivism' allied to ideas of 'race, empire and nation' (ibid.: 110), to the Fabian socialists of the radical left advocating a statist vision of 'regulated collectivism' in place of 'unregulated individualism' (ibid.: 112). Flanked on either side by these diametrically opposed, collectivist manoeuvres, liberalism was forced to adapt: to devise and adopt its own collectivist ideology, one that retained the idea of individual rights but couched in terms of social democracy. This *new* liberalism did not disarticulate the idea of individual liberties. Instead, it served to 'rearticulate classical liberalism within the imperatives of a collectivist and democratic age' (ibid.: 111).

The mutation of liberalism's philosophical and ideological DNA into the lexicon of new liberalism would have a notable impact on the evolution of the British political landscape: 'It was the language of new liberalism which then effectively defined the collectivist, social-democratic project in Britain for the next four or five decades' (ibid.: 116). From a feminist perspective, the restaging of liberalism in its 'social-democratic' guise was also influential in shaping twentieth-century, liberal-feminist strategies—strategies to work with and through the state with the aim of ameliorating women's rights and opportunities, as evidenced by the equality legislation achieved in the seventies.[1] In contrast to the individual liberties enshrined in 'old' liberalism, these legislative changes embraced a collectivist stance since they involved an awareness of *women's* oppression. As Eisenstein explains, a liberal feminism that 'demands' reform 'on behalf of women as a group' contradicts and moves beyond '"the principles of liberalism," which do not see people as groups, only individuals' (1981: 191). Feminism, she concludes, needs 'a social collectivity that recognises the independence and interconnectedness of women' (ibid.). But when an idea of individual autonomy separates from an understanding of 'interconnectedness', then feminism as a 'social-democratic' project comes undone. Neoliberalism's undoing of feminism rests on this very separation: the loss of a collectivist, socially orientated 'interconnectedness' and a strident re-articulation of liberalism's individualism.

Neoliberalism is new liberalism's nemesis. Highly antagonistic to the collectivist strategy that new liberalism maintained in the first half of the twentieth century, neoliberalism is ideologically, politically and economically opposed to the 'social-democratic' project. As outlined in Chapter 1, it was Thatcher who was determined on making neoliberalism hegemonic, a project that *New* Labour failed to redress. Equally, a new or third-way feminism vaunted women's power and freedom, exemplified by Natasha

Walter's *The New Feminism* in which an acknowledgement of persistent inequalities jostled alongside the recognition that 'individual women [were] also feeling powerful' and the idea that self-empowered women could 'join hands with one another, and with men, in order to make a more equal society in Britain' (Walter 1999: 221). Setting aside the sheer naivety of her proposal (the failure to acknowledge patriarchalism and the top-down approach by which women might empower other women less privileged than themselves), what Walter singularly failed to recognise is this: when the idea of the empowered, autonomous individual is configured within *anti-democratic* political conditions, then this increases the propensity to disconnect from any hand-holding with a socially democratic agenda.

Going into the twenty-first century, this is why the link Eisenstein insisted feminism needed to make between the 'independence' and the 'interconnectedness' of women as part of a 'social collectivity' was severed. Liberal feminism no longer registered the contradictory pull between the individualist creed of liberalism and social collectivism. Instead, co-opted by a neoliberal system, a liberal-feminist commitment to achieving equal opportunities for *all* women was re-written as the illiberal story of the individual, successful woman. This not only served to disarticulate the need for further equality-related struggles of the liberal-feminist kind, but also kept radical- and socialist-feminist forces in check. In brief, the political and cultural conditions of neoliberalism ensured a millennial mainstreaming of feminism's neoliberal double. Consequentially, as my open remarks attest, this has made it extremely difficult to recognise any political value in the liberal-feminist approach.

Moving Equality Centre Stage at the National?

Nonetheless, as outlined in Chapter 1, equality-focused feminism is on the move again as women theatre makers renew demands for more equal and diverse representation in the creative industries—demands that resonate with a sense of collectivity rather than individualism as equality is demanded on behalf of *all* women. Flagship institutions are under pressure to lead by example: to act for change in the expectation that this will have a beneficial ripple effect. And when a theatre is designated as a *national* theatre, there are equality questions to be asked about the gender and diversity of the nation it represents on its stages.

In the past, as regards British women playwrights, London's National Theatre appeared to operate a closed rather than open door 'policy'. I remember how it always felt like a landmark event when a premiere by one of our leading women dramatists such as Caryl Churchill, Sarah Daniels or Pam Gems made it as far as the smallest of the National's three stages (formerly the Cottesloe, now the Dorfman): *Neaptide* (Daniels, 1986), *The Skriker* (Churchill, 1994) and *Stanley* (Gems, 1996). You have to wait until 2008 for an original play by a contemporary woman playwright to be staged in the largest auditorium (the Olivier): Rebecca Lenkiewicz's *Her Naked Skin*. Equally, I can still recall my feelings of disappointment on watching the televised broadcast in 2013 of the National's celebration of *50 Years on Stage* (BBC2): fifty years, 'but where were the women playwrights?' as Catherine Love blogged at the time (2013). At the very least, I was foolishly hoping for a hint of Churchill. But as Love pointed out, only one of the scenes chosen for this gala event came from a work by a woman playwright: Alecky Blythe's musical *London Road*.

Since it was Rufus Norris who directed Blythe's *London Road* on the Cottesloe stage in 2011, an award-winning production that transferred to the Olivier auditorium, there were grounds for gender-related optimism when he succeeded Nicholas Hytner as Artistic Director of the National in 2015. Norris's programming stressed 'diversity', 'gender equality' and 'co-production' as important to increasing the theatre's audience demographic and to underpinning his aspirations for the venue 'to be national in terms of what we are debating, the subjects we are looking at, and particularly the people and stories we are representing' (quoted in Crompton 2015). Subsequently, Norris declared his commitment to achieving a 50:50 gender split among directors and playwrights by 2021; although a welcome declaration, at the time of writing, it looks unlikely that he will be able to deliver on his promise of gender parity.[2] Meanwhile, the doors of the Dorfman have admitted Wade and Raine, the two playwrights whose debut plays at the National reverberate with the unfinished histories of liberal feminism.[3]

Home, I'm Darling and the Resurrection of the 'Feminine Mystique'

Over the course of the last decade, I have been drawn to Wade as a writer whose comedic dramas keep a finger on the pulse of our neoliberal times: *Posh* (Royal Court, 2010; Duke of York's, 2012) her riotous critique of

Britain's elite class of young men destined for power; *Tipping the Velvet* (Lyric Hammersmith, 2015) an adaptation of Sarah Waters' novel that fused lesbian romance with a call to socialist arms. Behind the scenes, she fosters collaborations with women creatives. Lyndsey Turner who directed *Posh* worked with Wade on adapting *Tipping the Velvet*; Tamara Harvey, the director of *Home, I'm Darling* and Artistic Director of Theatr Clwyd, Wales, was a contemporary of Wade's at Bristol University and directed some of her early work (*Young Emma* and *16 Winters*). And the role of Judy in *Home, I'm Darling* was written for Katherine Parkinson who previously had appeared in Wade's online microplay *Britain isn't Eating* (*Guardian* and Royal Court, 2014).[4] Moreover, collaboration between the Welsh theatre and the National characterised the production process of *Home, I'm Darling*, for which a predominantly female team of creatives, including designer Anna Fleischle, worked together to render the vintage look of Wade's drama.

Between Fleischle's cutaway doll's house revealing upstairs and downstairs rooms and housewife Judy/Parkinson in glamorous, fifties frocks, it was hard not to miss the Ibsenite resonance, a quality that deepens as the drama unfolds and desperate housewife Judy conceals letters from the bank to prevent husband Johnny (Richard Harrington) learning of their mounting financial difficulties. Having said that, Wade inverts the liberal-feminist trope of the middle-class woman confined to domesticity and aspiring to life outside the doll's house by presenting Judy as a woman who retreats into the home as a refuge from the outside world of work and the pressures that accompany the dual role of managing a home and a career. Inversions and reversals underpin the politicising thrust of Wade's comedy from the motif of Judy as career-woman-turned-housewife to Johnny's objection to being recast in the role of patriarchal breadwinner. Judy's retro-fuelled fantasy does not stop at the front door of their suburban semi replete with fifties kitsch, from the humming retro fridge to the English Rose kitchen units. Rather, it conditions the couple's interactions with friends, family and the outside world: they promise each other not to go into the new shopping centre or dine out on pizza ('not very fifties', Wade 2018: 28) and are passionate about going to jive weekends in an Airstream that belongs to another couple, Fran (Kathryn Drysdale) and Marcus (Barnaby Kay), with whom they are close friends.

I readily admit that at the start of the show, as Johnny and Judy breakfasted together, I read the fifties set-up as for 'real'; my first impression was that Wade was locating her comedy in the decade characterised by the post-war settlement of gender roles and family values. But when Johnny left for work and Judy took out a laptop (her electronic portal to the consumption of vintage goods), it became clear that this was a fantasy of the fifties played out in the present. Playfully wrong-footed by Wade, I began to recognise her feminist engagement with the retro-imaging of the happy housewife. Fashioning herself as a happy homemaker, Judy overturns what Friedan uncovered in her classic, liberal-feminist text, *The Feminine Mystique*, as the unhappiness of the suburban housewife. Where Friedan sought to critique how domestic femininities were produced by the regulatory powers of the 'feminine mystique', Wade's Judy consumes and is consumed by the 'feminine mystique' as a happiness-making fantasy. She spends money, time and energy on styling the marital home with fifties memorabilia and accumulating an extensive wardrobe of fifties frocks (Parkinson had multiple costume changes). Consequentially, Judy's obsessive-compulsive restoration of the image of the happy housewife erases Friedan's feminist portrait of the unhappy, middle-class housewife, the cornerstone of her liberal-feminist thinking.

As Sara Ahmed observes, the restoration of the image of the happy housewife is a phenomenon that evidences not only women's discontents with the neoliberal workplace, but also the idea that feminism is seemingly to blame for encouraging women to abandon home as a happiness-making object. When '[t]he image of the happy housewife is repeated', Ahmed explains, it 'accumulates affective power in the very narration of her as a minority subject who has to reclaim something that has been taken from her' (2010: 53). I would not deny that there is an 'affective power' generated by Judy's re-occupation of the role of the housewife. I would be lying if I did not admit to moments of guilty pleasure over Parkinson's glamorous frocks, or the idea of days in which fancy, early-evening cocktails are a regular feature, especially when I think of the long-hours culture that shapes my academic life. Also, Parkinson's rendering of Judy made her such a likeable, affable character that at times a tiny contradictory part of me almost wanted her to succeed. But, overall, the greater 'affective power' of Wade's drama resides in the way it narrates how 'something [...] has been taken from' feminism when the doll's house returns as a popular women's fiction.

Judy's nostalgic longing for the rehabilitation of the happy-housewife-who-never-was is comically undercut throughout the play. Nobody feels at home in the 'gingham paradise' she has created (Wade 2018: 86); neither her husband, nor her friend Fran who is not in touch with her inner domestic goddess. The closest Fran comes to following a recipe during her working week is 'Pierce Film Lid' (ibid.: 9). The one exception is Fran's husband Marcus who is keen on the idea that his wife should follow Judy's example and give up her career as a stylist, but that is in character for a man who will later face an accusation of sexual harassment.

It is Judy's mother, Sylvia (Sian Thomas) who is most hostile to the 'gingham paradise' her daughter has fabricated. Sylvia's antagonism towards her daughter's domestic values stems from a life shaped by second-wave feminism and activism. She had hoped that her daughter would inherit her political outlook: 'All those years, all those pamphlets, marches. Ghastly rides to London in a minibus, hoping you'd get it by osmosis at least' (ibid.: 21). Judy insists that she is a feminist: is a woman who gets 'to choose' (ibid.). 'Wearing a frilly apron and dancing around with a duster isn't feminism', her mother counters (ibid.); 'You've made a luxury choice, don't pretend it's political' (ibid.: 22). In one way, this dialectical debate between mother and daughter reminds us of the long-standing polarisation between housewife and feminist: how difficult it is for the feminist and the housewife to be in the same room. In another, it directs us to the neoliberal mystique that enables Judy to re-fashion feminism as the individual woman's self-empowered right 'to choose'. Friedan explains that '[w]hen a mystique is strong, it makes its own fiction of fact. It feeds on the very facts which might contradict it, and seeps into every corner of culture' (2010 [1963]: 43). A neoliberal mystique 'feeds on' the social advances women have made to foster the fiction of women's freedom. This is a powerful fiction designed to conceal the contradiction between the idea that freedom has been granted and yet illiberal and patriarchal power relations remain firmly in place. And this is why the feminine 'I' who claims to choose is not a feminist subject: the 'I' who speaks from a subject-position enmeshed in the neoliberal mystique is the 'I' whose individualistic sense of entitlement entitles her to speak *as if* a feminist.

Sylvia makes just two appearances in the play, but each is pivotal to disarticulating her daughter's reclamation of the 'feminine mystique'. The first is when she challenges Judy's claims to feminism as previously described. On this occasion, she arrives uninvited at her daughter's home, seeking solace after attending the funeral of her feminist friend Erica who ran the commune in which she raised Judy after separating from her husband. Mourning the loss of her friend is symbolic of the 'passing' of second-wave feminism; we hear her taking comfort in the knowledge that, except for Judy, children of the commune have inherited socially progressive values.

In Act Two, Sylvia returns at the behest of her daughter since Judy wants to ask her for a loan from the money bequeathed to her from Erica. Sylvia refuses. Although probate is an issue (the money has not yet come through), it is the idea of her feminist friend's legacy being used to fund the doll's house that is the sticking point. From Sylvia's feminist perspective, the house is symbolic of an unreconstructed, patriarchal set-up (not least because funds from Judy's father were used for the house purchase and its fifties makeover). As mother and daughter are joined by Fran, anxious for company because she has just found out about an allegation of sexual harassment against Marcus, it is left to Sylvia to voice the patriarchal concerns the two younger women fail to acknowledge. And when Judy reassures Fran by saying the young woman accusing Marcus of sexual misconduct is possibly a 'fantasist' (Wade 2018: 86), Sylvia breaks into a monologic tirade against the fantasy life her daughter has constructed. This is the longest speech in the play and was delivered by Thomas in a resolute and matter-of-fact way to authenticate what the fifties were like to live through. For ordinary households, it was not colourful and glamorous as per Judy's makeover, but grey and dull. Houses were freezing; food was in short supply. The war had ended, but the world was 'broken' (ibid.: 87). Women had no control over their reproductive lives and there was no social tolerance: 'try being anything other than a straight white man and see if you think it's still utopia' (ibid.). By way of a codicil, Sylvia also debunks Judy's idolisation of her father: he was not a 'perfect 1950's gentleman', an amalgam of 'James Stewart and Gregory Peck', but a 'charismatic' philanderer (ibid.: 88).

Even without her mother's demolition of the suburban doll's house, the cracks in the facade of Judy's 'darling' home deepen to reveal its shaky foundations: the histories of liberal individualism and patriarchalism on which it was built—histories antithetical to women's 'freedom' as previously explained. On the one hand, individualism defined the culture of home ownership that underpinned the development of British suburbia. On the other, as Friedan observed in her North American context, suburbia was also highly gendered: segregated the urban city from the residential suburban outside; the masculine world of work from the feminine sphere of the domestic.[5] In short, the patriarchal construction of domesticated femininities provided the mortar for the bricks of bourgeois individualism. Thus, Judy's restoration of her fifties semi not only restores the patriarchalism of the 'feminine mystique' but also reclaims the values of bourgeois individualism foundational to the suburban archetype.

Wade brings home this point by contrasting Judy's lifestyle choice in her suburban semi with Sylvia's reminiscences of life in the commune. The latter rejected the idea of individualism by espousing an ethos of collectivism: a communal way of life with a daily diet of 'feminism and CND' (Wade 2018: 46) that was not at all to Judy's taste. The commune was housed in a '[b]ig run-down house out in the country near Brighton' (ibid.: 45). A dilapidated, rental property, outside of this coastal, gay-friendly city, signifies an alternative domestic arrangement: the reconstruction of the private sphere as one of shared parenting, communal dining and no cleaning. 'Nobody cleaned', Judy recalls, because everyone 'rejected the idea that their self-worth was linked to how much Hoovering they did' (ibid.: 46). Moreover, the rural location of the commune structures a feeling of retreat from life in the city, commonly associated with capitalism, even though, as Raymond Williams astutely observed in his seminal *The Country and the City*, the urban and the rural are both entangled in histories of capitalist production (Williams 1973).

City and country combine in the choice of Judy's suburban location of Welwyn Garden City in Hertfordshire, 20 miles outside of London. This is a highly considered choice on Wade's part: Welwyn Garden City was the second of two, interwar cities planned by Ebenezer Howard, founder of the Garden City movement (the first was Letchworth Garden City). Howard's planning was radical not only because his vision for Britain's new cities fused the urban and the rural, but also for the reason that there was a social dimension to his proposal: his solution to workers trapped in 'crowded, slum-infested cities' was for them to be included in and relocated to his community-orientated, garden-city scheme (Howard 1965 [1902]: 128). However, the issue of affordability militated against his socially inclusive designs.

A century later and the experiment of Judy and Johnny to turn the clocks back to Welwyn in its post-World War II incarnation as a new town for a new Britain also unravels. Just as the interwar, garden-city vista proved largely unaffordable for the working classes, without reserves of capital and/or a dual income in neoliberal Britain the leafy suburbs of Welwyn are well beyond the couple's means. As Joanne Hollows explains, 'an investment in elements of liberal feminism' such as education or a well-paid job may make middle-class women feel secure enough in their 'middle-class habitus' to choose 'domesticity over careers', but that sense of security also depends on 'significant reserves of economic capital' (Hollows 2006: 113). Judy does not have the economic freedom to make her 'luxury choice', exemplified by the way worsening financial circumstances force her to consider having sex with Marcus in exchange for a low-paid secretarial position in his firm. Her husband, on whom she is now totally financially dependent, cannot earn enough to fund their home and lifestyle.

Johnny's job in real estate is to sell the idea of home ownership. But the economic downturn in the age of neoliberal austerity (let us not forget that it was the subprime mortgage crisis in the US housing market that in 2007 precipitated the global banking crisis) makes it difficult for him to earn more commission and the promotion that would make the couple more financially secure. Wade's subplot featuring Johnny's female boss Alex (Sara Gregory) centres on Johnny's 'embattled masculinity' (2018: 106). His wife's project to make him 'feel like a man' (ibid.: 106) merely results in feelings of inadequacy and, ironically, prompts feelings for Alex whose company he finds more stimulating than that of his wife whose 'mind' and 'wit' 'have got lost in the house somehow' (ibid.: 105). He does not embark on an affair as Judy wrongly suspects, but his feelings for Alex lead him to insist that he and Judy review where their future happiness lies.

The climatic conundrum to which Wade's comedy builds revolves around this question of how to move forward when neither domesticity nor the workplace are constituted as happiness-making objects. Of course, for Friedan the liberal-feminist solution to the 'feminine mystique' was for greater numbers of women to choose careers over domestic entrapment, a solution for which she was often criticised since it both overlooked the numbers of women who were already working outside of the home and the domestic/work realities for women whose class and/or race situated them very differently to the fantasy of white, middle-class domestic unhappiness she critiqued (see Shriver 2010: xi). Furthermore, in the ensuing decades there was a critical connection that Eisenstein explains Friedan failed to make between the subsequent emergence of the 'superprofessional woman' who believed she could have it all (career and home) and the feminine homemakers of the fifties: *both* are manifestations of 'patriarchal ideology's manipulation of women's lives' (1981: 189). To which I would add that neopatriarchalism is entrenched in today's neoliberal mystique as Wade reflects in her empathetic rendering of Judy's discontent with the corporate workplace where she was more qualified but less valued than her male counterparts.

In her former top-girl life, Judy experienced quality leisure time as a commodity in very short supply. Her working week meant 'leaving the office at seven and racing home to find [Johnny] eating crisps and frowning into the fridge' (Wade 2018: 65). As Beatrix Campbell observes, the 'power to *take* women's time is a resource for both patriarchy and capitalism' (2013: 20, original emphasis). Even though 'the old sexual settlement is *un*settled, unsustainable, it is reinstated: women's presence in the world of waged work is permanent yet always contingent on *taking care of care*' (ibid.; original emphasis). However, as Judy settles for a life consisting entirely of '*taking care of care*', this translates into spending days isolated from any sense of community (she never leaves the house) and succumbing to the mind-numbing, daily rhythms of cleaning, tidying and cooking.[6] Time spent on preparing fresh food, gardening and growing vegetables does yield ecological value. But the time Judy spends on such activities is contradicted by the energy costs of running a vintage car for Johnny or their high-maintenance retro fridge. Equally, there is the absurdity of time wasted on decanting food products into fifties containers or polishing the cutlery in the middle of the night. And there is the time-trap of a day spent waiting for Johnny's return from the office—waiting filled with anxious thoughts about the affair he is not guilty of. Or, there is the ritual of cocktail drinking whose scheduling gets earlier by the day for the woman who finds she has too much time on her hands.

What then *is* the solution when the double demands on women's labour, time and energy have intensified in our age of neoliberal austerity, and the fantasy of going home merely sounds the retreat into 'a white bourgeois fantasy of the past, a nostalgia for a past that was never possible as a present for most women, let alone being available in the present' (Ahmed 2010: 52)? A 'feminist politics of time' (Campbell 2013: 20) calls for a rebalancing of the time spent on domestic caretaking and in the workplace. In her wordless coda to *Home, I'm Darling*, Wade offers the moving image (in all senses) of Judy and Johnny in their kitchen, both preparing to leave home for the office. They have not given up on their fifties image, but they have toned it down. Parkinson/Judy is no longer attired in a full-skirted frock (so full that it takes up an inordinate about a space, creating distance between her body and those around her).

She has swapped it for formal '*1950s-style office wear*' (Wade 2018: 110). Unlike the opening scene in which Judy waits on Johnny at breakfast, the couple's breakfasting is a shared routine; when they depart for work, Parkinson/Judy briefly pauses to look back at the house standing empty and alone. Her affective bond with her 'darling' home, the signifier of choice feminism, is broken.

Where Wade leaves us with Judy's alternate identification with an egalitarian mode of shared domestic work and labour as a utopian imaging of what equality might feel and look like, Raine sets out to explore a further dimension to equality: the idea of consensual sexual relations.

Consent in Conversation with *Eve Was Shamed*

Raine is a dramatist who excels at conveying the power relations produced through the command, or lack thereof, of language. In *Rabbit* (Old Red Lion Theatre, 2006) a cacophony of young professionals ruminating on their futures contrasts with a father whose illness means he is losing the capacity to speak, and *Tribes* (Royal Court Theatre, 2010) detonates familial fireworks when a deaf son brought up to lip-read learns sign-language. In *Tiger Country* (Hampstead Theatre, 2011) which Raine also directed, she turned the spotlight on a national institution: wove a multi-layered, fast-paced narrative of an ailing and hierarchically run National Health Service in which senior female medics struggle to have their say. No less multi-layered, *Consent* opens a window on to the UK's legal system: cross-examines its purported neutrality by revealing the maldistribution of justice as women plaintiffs in rape trials are silenced by the weight of judicial authority.

Reforming the law, legislating for change to enhance women's rights, is a defining feature of liberal feminism, one that highlights the paradox of women's petitioning of a liberal state whose political lawmakers and judiciary have denied them those very rights. We might think again of that image of suffragette militancy, of women protesting their rights outside of Westminster, and then reflect that women won the right to vote; that a century later there are women MPs who sit *inside* the parliament building and more women 'in the law and on the Bench' (Kennedy 2018: 11). If this feels like progress of sorts, then we must also reflect that the liberal-feminist strategy of women gaining increased access to institutions that wield power has its limitations. In a worst-case scenario, this paves the way for the top-girl syndrome and 'equality by domination' (see Chapter 1) in which privileged men *and* women exercise economic, political or judicial power to uphold a masculinist and corporate neoliberal imagination. We are no further forward on the equality front when the woman who gains entry to the boys' establishment embraces power at the expense of other women. On the other hand, women (and men) working through institutional vectors of power towards social democracy and justice can help to remedy inequalities and injustices. As Chantal Mouffe argues regarding neoliberal parliamentary power characterised by a failure to radicalise democracy, the solution does not lie in 'abolishing representation but in making our institutions *more representative*' (Mouffe 2018: 57; emphasis added).

One woman who has been at the forefront of making the judicial system 'more representative' is Helena Kennedy QC who contributed an essay to the programme notes for the National's production of *Consent*. In 2018 as *Consent* transferred to the Harold Pinter Theatre in the West End, Kennedy published *Eve Was Shamed*, her second monograph on how women are unfairly treated by the British legal system. In her introductory chapter, Kennedy refers to her earlier book, *Eve Was Framed* (1992), to describe how that project was 'highly contentious, especially within the profession and among the judiciary', but was welcomed by women who recognised themselves and their experiences in her account of 'the law's failure to provide justice for women' (Kennedy 2018: 2). If the notes of thanks Kennedy received from women 'seemed like a victory' (ibid.), it was a hollow victory: *Eve Was Shamed* once again puts the UK's legal system on trial for continuing to fail women.

If equality is the goal, then what, Kennedy asks, is equality: 'What does it look like? What kind of equality do we want? And how might the law help in achieving it?' (ibid.: 13). If equality involves more women in powerful positions, women 'who learn to exercise power just as men do is not going to achieve real equality' (ibid.). For 'real equality', Kennedy suggests we should imagine a world in which there is no patriarchal control and power over women's lives; where equal pay is a reality but there is no need to work excessively long hours; and a world in which what Campbell describes as 'the taking care of care' does not overburden women. And equality also 'means true and consensual sexual relations' (ibid.: 13).

As Raine's title indicates, 'consensual sexual relations' is the play's major theme. *Consent* is set in the middle-class milieu of two couples: Edward (Ben Chaplin) and Kitty (Anna Maxwell Martin), Rachel

(Priyanga Burford) and Jake (Adam James). Both couples are representative of high-earning, early-parenting households: Edward, Rachel and Jake work in the legal profession; Kitty is in publishing, though on maternity leave following the birth of their first child.[7] Rachel and Jake have two young children. Over the course of the play, the private lives of the couples will prove every bit as adversarial as the law and infidelities will pull both marriages apart.

The twinning of domestic and courtroom dramas was visually underscored in Hildegard Bechtler's design. In contrast to the single-set, doll's house construction replete with fifties furnishings in *Home, I'm Darling*, *Consent* was staged on a low platform; a dazzling array of pendant lights was suspended over the space and furniture was mechanically raised from the floor to accommodate the locational shifts from bourgeois interiors to courtroom. *Home I'm Darling* made an impression by eliciting contradictory feelings on my part: the guilty pleasures of frocks and cocktails in tension with the feminist recognition that equality was not be found in the bourgeois fantasy of domestic retreat. *Consent*, directed by Roger Michell, left impressions of quarrelling couples whose choice of weapon is the witty putdown, barbed comment, or line of contempt for whoever is perceived to be the guilty partner. After listening to the play's two-act, quartet of antagonistic, marital voices, I came away with the sense of marriage among the affluent middle classes as something of a miscarriage of justice.

Marital meltdown begins with Kitty and Jake: infidelity on Jake's part leads to separation and the threat of divorce. Reconciliation is achieved by the close of the first act, but only to be mirrored by Edward and Kitty's split in the second. However, the symmetry of the break-ups is altered by a gender reversal: it is Kitty who has embarked on a relationship with Edward's friend and work colleague, Tim (Pip Carter). Cross-examined by her husband, Kitty cites her motive for the affair as payback for Edward cheating on her five years previously: '*I wanted you to understand how it felt*' (Raine 2017: 85).[8] Before the play closes, Kitty, having left Edward but been abandoned by Tim, meets with her estranged husband. Together, they fold a dustcover in the house that stands empty waiting to be sold, a repetition of tablecloth folding seen in the opening scene. Reconciliation hovers over the action of folding as Edward who feels sorry for Kitty explains, 'I do know what you must feel like. I know what it feels like now. I know how much it hurts' (ibid.: 113).

I have thought since about this question of hurting as reminiscent of John Osborne's *Look Back in Anger*. Except, of course, in Osborne's play the roles were reversed: it was the angry young man, Jimmy Porter, who wanted his wife Alison to feel and to hurt, and it was Alison who returned home after a miscarriage to play the intimate game of squirrels and bears with the husband whose misogynistic, abusive behaviour had driven her away. 60 years later, does reverse gender behaviour imply equality? When women emulate men's behaviour by cheating, want men to feel how hurting feels and to get even, is this what equality looks like? Clearly, getting even does not translate into equality. Rather, Kitty's act of infidelity, or Rachel's settling of marital scores by giving a male friend a blowjob to teach Jake a lesson, are reprisals on the part of the women which signify that when men regard marriage as a licence to cheat, this is not the idea of marriage the women consented to.

Casting Kitty and Rachel as women determined on vengeance and in both cases threatening to deny their husbands access to their children, gestures to a genealogical connection to Greek drama and its array of unruly women who were subjected to patriarchy and yet resistant to the abuses of male power (see Chapter 3 on *The Suppliant Women*). 'Before you mistreat your women, remember what they're capable of', cautions Zara (Daisy Haggard), an actress and old friend of Kitty's, to her assembled 'audience' of Kitty, Edward, Jake and Tim (ibid.: 25). Zara, who happens to be appearing as Medea in what sounds like a ghastly avant-garde production, is referring to the Greek tragedy. But of course, her description sounds like a harbinger of things to come (murmurs of recognition among the National's audience). As the conversation pivots to theatre, then comes Tim's definition of a 'classic Greek play': 'Two opposing characters holding two relative but mutually destructive truths' (ibid.: 26). What might be stated of Greek drama also applies to the dramaturgy of the courtroom. And an agonistic principle also determines the structure of Raine's play: husbands and wives self-destructively compete for their version of marital events to be recognised as *the* truth.

Raine spent a lot of time in the company of barristers and attending court cases, immersing herself in procedures and legalistic discourse.[9] She was struck by the way in which barristers talk about their case in the first person: 'I've been raping pensioners', Jake explains '*wearily*' to the others in the opening scene (ibid.: 13). This is the first time we hear this disjunctive device: the middle-class professional speaking as the criminal 'I'. Other instances follow in quick succession: Rachel is on a murder case and Kitty asks, 'who have *you* murdered?', while Edward is also involved in a 'spot of rape' (ibid.: 14). It is an arresting, darkly humorous technique that belongs to a world most of us are not familiar with (other than our television screens) and a reminder of the prevalent social gap between those whose professional role is to act on behalf of others and those whom they represent:

> *Kitty*: You say 'I' and 'we' when you're defending them but it's not, it's *them*, isn't it?
> *Edward*: Yes, it's them, and so what? We're *not* them! That's why we're paid to *argue* for them – because they can't string two fucking words together! (ibid.: 70)[10]

Accustomed to speaking for/as 'them', Edward and Jake are contrastingly less adept at defending their own guilty behaviours (Edward's historic affair; Jake's current affairs). Emotionally distraught at the prospect of losing their wives and especially their children, neither man can see reason in his wife's behaviour. Feeling guilty about her own behaviour, Kitty willingly comforts (hugs) Edward but begins to resist when this intimacy turns sexual: 'No. It's too late' (ibid.: 87). At this crucial juncture, the lights dimmed and the scene ended; as an audience, we were not privy to what happened next. Instead, the dramatic pause on this event was followed by animated debate between Edward, Jake and Rachel concerning Kitty's subsequent accusation of rape.

'Where does seduction end and rape begin?' (Kennedy 2018: 114). 'A "no" may be taken for granted when a respectable woman is attacked by a stranger in a dimly lit street', but because 'the vast majority of rapes are committed by men known to the victim, consent in rape trials has always been an issue which makes men very nervous' (ibid.). A 'classic case of marital rape' is Jake's verdict after listening to Edward's account (Raine 2017: 93). But there appears to be nothing 'classic' or clear-cut about it: 'Did you ask her for consent?', Rachel asks Edward (ibid.: 92). 'Oh for God's sake, of course not! She's ... my... we're...It was...nonverbal. It was *sex*', Edward self-justifies (ibid.). The question of consent is hotly debated among the couples in Act 2 sc. 4 (although Kitty, like Rachel in the parallel scene in Act 1, separates herself from the others). In another of Raine's gender reversals, it is Rachel who sees Edward's point of view; Jake who takes Kitty's side.[11] Edward insists the sex was a 'mercy fuck'; Kitty protests she 'said "no", several times' (ibid.: 100) and reminds Rachel that she 'always say[s] there can't be *degrees* of rape' (ibid.: 101). 'There's a world in which you're *both* telling the truth', Jake reflects, 'But that's not the *law*. In court, your narratives are oil and water. They can never mix' (ibid.: 99). Only one truth can prevail.

That women's veracity about rape is less likely to be believed in court remains a depressingly familiar story. The reporting of rapes has increased but the 'conviction rate for rape in Britain is still the lowest for all serious crime' (Kennedy 2018: 113).[12] Moreover, the uncovering of Jimmy Savile's serial abuse of women and children (see Chapter 1) saw an increase in the reporting of *historic* cases of abuse, harassment or rape. Yet Raine depicts her lawyers as highly antipathetic to historic rape cases: no evidence, argues Edward, and 'it seems like *anyone* can have a go, bringing it up *now* as an alibi for their failed life' (Raine 2017: 69).

This misogynistic view brings me to one further narrative layer in *Consent* that is crucial to showing how the liberal-feminist goal of achieving equality in law is not in itself enough: an end to patriarchy is also essential if the legal system is to become 'more representative'. I have reserved this layer of *Consent* until last to make my own case for Raine's restaging of what many feminists of all stripes recognise 'to be the whole truth and nothing but the truth': women who come forward as rape victims are more often than not shamed and failed by the justice system.

There is one more character in the play who, like Tim and Zara, functions as an outsider[13]: rape victim, Gayle, a role that doubles with that of a solicitor, Laura; both were played by Heather Craney. Where Raine portrays acts of revenge and betrayal that criss-cross the sexes, in her conception of Gayle she unequivocally takes the woman's part by depicting her as a woman who puts the legal system on trial for its failure to secure a conviction against the man who beyond all reasonable doubt raped her.

As noted in Chapter 1, it was Kimberlé Crenshaw who advocated the term intersectionality to address the sexist *and* racist discrimination black women face; her advocacy for an intersectional framework was based on evidence of the American courts' failure to recognise and support compound axes of discrimination in their judicial findings and judgements (Crenshaw 1989). In today's British courts, Kennedy observes that the 'intersectionality of discrimination' persists: 'multiplies the effects of gender discrimination when coupled with racism and class disadvantage and contempt for any person who is different' (2018: 11–12). And Raine testifies to the combined effects of class and gender discrimination by showing Gayle as a working-class woman who is held in contempt. She is one of 'them': a woman without means, '*cheaply but smartly dressed*' (Raine 2017: 19). Craney's inexpensive-looking outfit—a splash of pink jacket over a dark ensemble and black heels—discriminated her from the besuited and gowned prosecuting barrister (Tim/Carter) and defence for the accused (Edward/Chaplin). Equally her Scottish identity sets her apart from the affluent London set: to the ear of the male legal whose RP speech denotes social capital and authority, Gayle's Scottish accent conveys inferiority; Tim and especially Edward stereotype her as a woman of lower class and lesser intelligence. In Edward's eyes, Gayle is a 'pisshead', a woman who 'liked a bit of rough' (ibid.: 49), a woman who loses her case because his 'rapist just performed a lot better' (ibid.: 50).

To show why it is that a woman who is deeply traumatised by being raped on the day of her sister's funeral is not believed in court, Raine marshals her extensive research to show the multiple factors that come into prejudicial play. A commanding figure in the cross-examination scene (Act 1 sc. 4), Chaplin/Edward undermined Gayle's credibility. How much had Gayle been drinking (unsuitable behaviour for a woman)? And what about her seeing a therapist (must be mentally unstable). Or her phone-text reply to the rapist the morning after to tell him she was fine (no case to answer, surely). What does not get heard in court are the reasons for the therapy and the text message: counselling for a double rape that happened to Gayle and her sister ten years ago; the text message sent because she knew her rapist had violently assaulted a friend of hers. 'That's why I *answered* his fucking text. I didne want him to come *back* and do *me* in' (ibid.: 77).[14] Furthermore, the rapist's past was not allowed to be heard in court, the judge 'decided he would be tried on the facts of the case alone' (ibid.).

These explanations only come out when Gayle has tracked down Edward at his home to put her side of the story. In the final, climactic scene to the first act, she gate-crashes the Christmas party Edward and Kitty are hosting. The irony of what she sees does not escape her: the middle-class set getting drunk and illegally smoking weed; Edward and Tim behaving as mates rather than adversaries. The question of feeling and hurting arises again; Gayle wants Edward to feel something of what she feels—the knowledge that an unwelcome somebody knows how to find you. '*Patrick Taylor* [the rapist] knows where *I* live. So now you know what it feels like, eh?' (ibid.: 78). And above all she wants Edward to know that what he did to her in court was 'criminal' (ibid.: 79).

Even when the Crown Prosecution Service decides there is enough evidence for a rape to go to trial, many women do not proceed since they know that in court they are likely to feel abused all over again. This is a well-known, widely reported phenomenon (see Kennedy 2018: 140), but a relatively unknown fact is that a victim is not appointed a lawyer. As Raine describes: 'The thing that really shocked and surprised me when researching the play was the fact that in a rape trial the victim does not have a lawyer allocated to him or her. So a barrister is prosecuting the rapist, he is not defending the victim – so there's no one to actually stand up and defend the victim' (Raine, n.d.). This was a revelation to me as well; in my re-reading of the play, I kept going back to the first courtroom scene (Act 1 sc. 2) in which Gayle tries to understand how things work, thinking again about how the system feels so one-sided. 'Are you the one on my side then?', a bewildered Gayle asks Tim, who explains that 'strictly speaking' he is acting for the crown and that 'technically' Gayle is a 'witness' (ibid.: 20). And yet another thing I did not know is revealed in this scene: a prosecutor cannot talk to the victim about events since this would constitute coaching. As Kennedy observes, it makes for a 'process' that 'seems remote and unconcerned with the woman's feelings' (2018: 141).

To reinstate Gayle's credibility as a victim/witness, Raine gives the final word to Gayle in each of the three scenes in which she appears. To Tim, ill-prepared for the case and cutting off the conversation about the rape, Gayle states firmly and definitively, 'He raped me' (Raine 2017: 22). At the end of Edward's cross-examination, Craney/Gayle addressed the audience as her jury: 'He raped me on the day of my little sister's funeral. He came into my bedroom in the middle of the night and raped me. And I will look at him, there, and say it' (ibid.: 42). Also, the party scene ends with Gayle's revelation of the earlier rape and a refusal to be comforted by Kitty. Raine does not show what happens to her thereafter: following the Greek convention of keeping violent acts offstage, what is reported in the second act is Gayle's suicide. Although I recognise the dramaturgical logic of this decision, from a feminist perspective this marginalisation of the already marginalised does feel problematic since the working-class, female outsider has no further opportunity to make her case.

That said, Gayle's suicide does disturb Kitty and Edward's middle-class contentment; Kitty identifies it as the reason why she and Edward grew apart. After Gayle hanged herself, Edward retreated into work and 'that's when it all started to go wrong', she explains to the divorce lawyer,

Laura (ibid.: 96). Playing the part of Laura after the role of Gayle, Craney embodied the schizophrenic split between the woman who was shamed and failed by the legal system and the professional who simultaneously advises Kitty *and* Edward on whether either of them has a case (she swivelled between them on an office chair). Craney's execution of this short scene heightened the sense of irony in the doubling: performing the detached and dispassionate professional, she had little interest in either Kitty's or Edward's emotionally driven arguments.

Edward complains that he does not 'believe in argument any more, I don't think people listen to argument, rationality and logic – they just *decide* and that's that' (ibid.: 69). However, *Consent* is a drama that demands spectators listen to argument and weigh up the evidence, an intellectual process that because of the play's subject is likely to stir up feelings when individually held beliefs and views are upheld or contested. As *Guardian* reviewer Michael Billington observed, this is a play that 'stimulates debate rather than stifles it' (2017).

Closing Argument

As a drama that 'stimulates debate', *Consent* belongs to the well-established tradition of a theatre of ideas, exemplified by the late nineteenth-century thesis play of which Ibsen's *A Doll's House* is a seminal example. In recent times, critical and theoretical attentions to experimental forms, notably of the post-dramatic kind, have devalued drama that adheres to conventions of narrative and character and works through ideas that connect to the outside world. Yet the success of *Home, I'm Darling* as a contemporary inversion of *A Doll's House* and *Consent* with its multi-layered deliberations over consensual sex suggests audiences do have an appetite for theatre that stages urgent social questions. As Billington reflects, there may well be a correlation between the public's loss of faith in the political deliberations of Westminster (now exemplified by the Brexit crisis) and the turn to theatre as an artistic forum for 'provocative debate about the society we inhabit' (2014).

Furthermore, the ideas play is never only a question of ideas: it is the theatrical rendering of the ideas that is crucial to stimulating debate. As the performance analysis in this chapter reflects, my interpretation of ideas was informed by the theatrical rendering of key images (the absurdity of an over-dressed Parkinson/Judy in the fifties kitchen) or words that left a notable impression (Thomas's emphatic denunciation of Judy's 'luxury choice'). Equally, there were moments of affective realisation that occurred through the process of researching and reading: the shock of not knowing that technically a rape victim has no lawyer on her side, or the renewed sense of injustice that arose during my re-readings of *Consent* post-Weinstein.[15] I would also like to think or hope that the critical reflections in this chapter might stimulate feminist identifications with or further debate about Wade's critique of choice feminism and Raine's idea about inequality before the law.

Kennedy reminds us that the 'law mirrors society' and 'reflects' all its inequalities (2018: 18). It not only 'reflects' but also 'affects' ideas about 'the subordination and lesser status of women', which is why, from her feminist perspective, 'all of those involved in the administration of justice have a special obligation to reject society's irrational prejudices' (ibid.). That 'obligation' is recognised by playwrights and creatives who mobilise theatre's capacity to reflect inequalities and social injustices and to affect perceptions about the 'society we inhabit'. Wade's comedy of ideas refuses to endorse the view that occupation neoliberal housewife is a recipe for women's liberation; neoliberal mystique and its appropriation of liberal-feminist discourse to vaunt the 'freedom fallacy' is subjected to a comedically realised social critique. *Consent's* multi-layered exposé of the law and the prejudicial attitudes of those who administer it testifies that equality cannot be achieved when the neoliberal state upholds the 'law' of patriarchy.

It is only at the limits of what can be achieved by liberal-feminist reform that the necessity for more socially transformative feminisms comes into view. What Chapter 3 will show is that patriarchy is being fiercely contested by today's feminists: a re-awakening of radical-feminist sensibilities is moving women's long-standing struggle against patriarchalism centre stage.

Notes

1. The Equal Pay Act was passed in 1970 and came into force under the Sex Discrimination Act 1975.
2. In March 2019 when the National announced its new season of six plays, all of them by men and only one directed by a woman, Sandi Toksvig wrote a letter of feminist outrage and complaint to Norris that was widely

circulated in the press. See Bird (2019) for Toksvig's letter and Norris' response.

3. Other significant, original new works by British women playwrights to be staged in the Dorfman during Norris' tenure include Churchill's *Here We Go* (Lyttleton 2015); *Mosquitoes* by Lucy Kirkwood (2017); *Nine Night* (2018) by Natasha Gordon (see Chapter 1); and Raine's *Stories* (2018). Notable revivals by women writers include: *Cleansed* (Dorfman 2016), the first NT production of a play by the late Sarah Kane; Churchill's *Light Shining in Buckinghamshire* (Lyttleton 2015); and Timberlake Wertenbaker's *Our Country's Good* (Olivier 2016).
4. *Britain isn't Eating* can be viewed at https://www.theguardian.com/stage/video/2014/nov/17/britain-isnt-eating-microplay-guardian-royal-court-video.
5. For a discussion of suburban development, see Harris and Larkham (1999); on gender and suburbia, see Strong-Boag et al. (1999).
6. Wade depicts Judy as a woman who has no designs on having children. That way she avoids representing the idea of maternal time as the 'natural' or preferred option for the woman who gives up her career. It also heightens the absurdity of the marital home as woman's *raison d'être.*
7. Raine's own baby made an appearance in the opening sequence as Edward and Kitty's new arrival. Listening to Jenni Murray's interview with Raine and Kennedy on *Woman's Hour* broadcast on BBC Radio 4, 13 April 2017, I discovered that I was by no means the only spectator to be delightfully distracted by the question of whether the baby was real or not; he was so extraordinarily pacific!
8. Italics here and in all citations from Raine's *Consent* are in the original.
9. In Act 1 sc. 6 in which Edward and Tim coach Zara for an acting role as a barrister, Raine depicts many of the verbal tricks and techniques lawyers use in the courtroom.
10. We also hear about Rachel and Jake's oldest son Jimmy referring to himself as 'you' rather than 'I'. Having just got the 'hang of calling himself "I"', he has started saying 'I didn't see me doing that' when he wants to say he cannot remember what he has done (Raine 2017: 45). Rachel makes a parenthetical observation about Jake as the father who cannot remember the person he was or recognise what he has done to their marriage.
11. In Rachel and Jake's break-up, Kitty takes Rachel's side and Edward defends Jake.
12. Kennedy calculates that in the last ten years, the rate of conviction is a shockingly low 7% (2018: 113).
13. Tim and Zara are the singletons who disturb middle-class coupledom. Tim, joked about by all the others as a man who smells and looks like a hamster, is the unlikely object of first Zara's and then Kitty's sexual attention, but each woman has an ulterior motive: Kitty's is revenge; Zara

desperately wants a baby. When Kitty takes up with Tim and betrays Zara, Edward is reportedly willing to father a child for Zara. However, this incestuous revenge saga completes by Tim losing interest in Kitty and returning to Zara.

14. Kennedy explains: 'One of the serious problems for women is that their own phones, computers and tablets can often provide material that can be used evidentially to undermine their credibility' (2018: 119).
15. Raine observed that by the time of *Consent's* post-Weinstein, West End revival there was 'an extra vibration humming through' the play (Raine, n.d.).

Works Cited

Ahmed, S. 2010. *The Promise of Happiness*. Durham, London: Duke University Press.

Billington, M. 2014. Speaking Truth to Power: This Is the Rebirth of Political Theatre. *Guardian*, 7 November. https://www.theguardian.com/commentisfree/2014/nov/07/rebirth-political-theatre-society-stage.

———. 2017. Love and Justice on Trial in Fierce Courtroom Drama. *Guardian*, 5 April. https://www.theguardian.com/stage/2017/apr/05/consent-review-nina-raine-dorfman-london-anna-maxwell-martin.

Bird, S. 2019. National Theatre Should Change Its Name After 'Ignoring' Women, Sandi Toksvig Says. *Telegraph*, 30 March. https://www.telegraph.co.uk/news/2019/03/30/national-theatre-should-change-name-ignoring-women-sandi-toksvig/.

Campbell, B. 2013. *End of Equality: The Only Way Is Women's Liberation*. London: Seagull.

Crenshaw, K. 1989. Demarginalizing the Intersection of Race and Sex: A Black Feminist Critique of Antidiscrimination Doctrine, Feminist Theory and Antiracist Politics. *University of Chicago Legal Forum* 1 (8): 139–167.

Crompton, S. 2015. Interview, Rufus Norris: How the National Needs to Change. *Guardian*, 25 September. https://www.theguardian.com/stage/2015/sep/25/rufus-norris-first-national-theatre-season-interview.

Eisenstein, Z.R. 1981. *The Radical Future of Liberal Feminism*. New York: Longman.

Friedan, B. 2010 [1963]. *The Feminine Mystique*. London: Penguin.

Hall, S., and B. Schwarz. 1988. State and Society, 1880–1930. In *Thatcherism and the Crisis of the Left: The Hard Road to Renewal*, S. Hall, 95–122. London: Verso.

Harris, R., and P.J. Larkham. 1999. Suburban Foundation, Form and Function. In *Changing Suburbs: Foundation, Form and Function*, ed. R. Harris and P.J. Larkham, 1–31. London: E & FN Spon.

Hollows, J. 2006. Can I Go Home Yet? Feminism, Post-feminism and Domesticity. In *Feminism in Popular Culture*, ed. J. Hollows and R. Moseley, 97–118. Oxford: Berg.

Howard, E. 1965 [1902]. *Garden Cities of To-Morrow*, ed. F.J. Osborn. London: Faber.

Kennedy, H. 2018. *Eve Was Shamed: How British Justice Is Failing Women*. London: Chatto & Windus.

Kiraly, M., and M. Tyler, eds. 2015. *Freedom Fallacy: The Limits of Liberal Feminism*. Ballarat: Connor Court.

Love, C. 2013. Great Gala, But Where Were the Women Writers? *WhatsOnStage*, 4 November. https://www.whatsonstage.com/london-theatre/news/catherine-love-great-gala-but-where-were-the-women_32534.html.

Mouffe, C. 2018. *For a Left Populism*. London: Verso.

Raine, N. n.d. Nina Raine on *Consent*. National Theatre Blog. https://www.nationaltheatre.org.uk/blog/nina-raine-consent.

———. 2017. *Consent*. London: Nick Hern.

Shriver, L. 2010. Introduction. In *The Feminine Mystique*, B. Friedan, v–xi. London: Penguin.

Strong-Boag, V., I. Dyck, K. England, and L. Johnson. 1999. What Women's Spaces? Women in Australian, British, Canadian and US Suburbs. In *Changing Suburbs: Foundation, Form and Function*, ed. R. Harris and P.J. Larkham, 168–186. London: E & FN Spon.

Wade, L. 2018. *Home, I'm Darling*. London: Oberon.

Walter, N. 1999. *The New Feminism*. London: Virago.

Williams, R. 1973. *The Country and the City*. St. Albans, Herts: Paladin.

CHAPTER 3

Acting Together: A Chorus of Radical-Feminist Protest

Abstract This chapter stages a re-encounter with the histories, legacies and renewals of radical feminism. In the context of the #Me Too Movement and the post-Weinstein watershed, it argues women's renewed identification with the radical-feminist goal to end an injurious patriarchal system. Analysis of the anti-patriarchal dynamic of #Me Too as affectively rendered dissensual speech serves to develop feminist-theatre reflections on the importance of affect in the formation of political attachments. Chantal Mouffe's Spinozan-informed concept of the artistic 'production of ideas with the power to affect' is taken up in two case studies: David Greig's version of *The Suppliant Women* and Morgan Lloyd Malcolm's all-female production of *Emilia*.

Keywords Radical feminism · Patriarchy · #Me Too · Ideas, affections and affects · Intersectionality and the all-female production

On 28 February 2006, I attended a reading of Sarah Daniels' *Masterpieces* presented under the umbrella of the Royal Court Theatre's fiftieth-anniversary celebrations. First staged in 1983, *Masterpieces* dramatises a radical-feminist outcry against the pornography industry and a misogynist culture. It was a play that originally stimulated fierce debate among audiences and produced an anti-radical-feminist rant on the part of many male critics. Listening to the reading, I felt *Masterpieces* had not lost its power to voice a radical-feminist critique of the damaging effects of male

E. Aston, *Restaging Feminisms*,
https://doi.org/10.1007/978-3-030-40589-2_3

violence against women, ranging from misogynist joke-telling to the snuff movie. But it was the post-show discussion led by Daniels that lingered most in my memory of the event—a talk in which women from different generations articulated attachments to the play's radical-feminist subject matter. In brief, what emerged from the inter-generational responses to *Masterpieces* was an overriding sense that women's objections to a misogynist culture were not confined to the feminist past but were being revitalised by a widely shared recognition of engrained patriarchalism. Thus, looking back, I think of this feminist-theatre event as an early indicator of what would later emerge as an upsurge of opposition to an entrenched culture of sexism.

As described in Chapter 2, a neoliberal mystique enmeshed in patriarchalism needs to suppress counter-hegemonic tendencies that contest its hegemonic power. It makes an ally of choice feminism to disarticulate the democratic aspirations and designs of socially progressive modes of feminism. Hence, as Angela McRobbie explains, the millennial mainstreaming of choice feminism evidenced women as 'disempowered through the very discourses of empowerment [...] offered as substitutes for feminism' (2009: 49). Consequently, such 'substitutes' rendered third-way feminist ideas of empowerment erroneous; Natasha Walter, who vaunted the notion of 'new feminism' conceded she 'was entirely wrong' about how 'remnants of old-fashioned sexism' would 'wither away' (2015 [2010]: 8). In a marked contrast to her earlier, hubristic voicing of 'new feminism', she observed: 'The rise of a hypersexual culture is not proof that we have reached full equality; rather, it has reflected and exaggerated the deeper imbalances of power in our society' (ibid.).

However, those 'deeper imbalances of power' occasioned the realization of a worsening patriarchalism. Launched in 2012, Laura Bates' 'Everyday Sexism' project provided an online forum and outlet for the hidden injuries of sexism. Akin to the spectrum of male violence against women dramatised in *Masterpieces*, the 'Everyday Sexism' site registered instances of violence ranging from misogynist joke-telling, through sexual harassment on the street and in the workplace, to crimes of domestic violence and rape. As women uploaded their individual stories and experiences of sexism, the overall effect ignited recognition of a patriarchal culture oppressive to 'women of all ages, races and ethnicities, of different social backgrounds, gender identities and sexual orientations' (Bates 2014: 18). All told, revelation after revelation of 'everyday sexism' and the persistent abuses of male power prophesied the outcry precipitated by the Weinstein scandal. As Helena Kennedy puts it, what the Weinstein watershed generated was the need 'to become more confident in naming … [patriarchy] as one of the main blights on all our lives'—especially women's lives given that '[p]atriarchy while expressing admiration for femininity actually holds it in contempt' (2018: 7, 8). A feminist interrogation of an injurious patriarchalism structures and flows through this restaging radical feminism chapter as I consider the counter-hegemonic, anti-patriarchal voicings resonant in #Me Too and productions of David Greig's version of Aeschylus' *The Suppliant Women* (2016) and Morgan Lloyd Malcolm's *Emilia* (2018).

Revisiting Radical Feminism

Kennedy explains that when she wrote *Eve Was Framed* (see Chapter 2), she avoided using the term patriarchy principally because of its negative connotations as a 'hostile ideology' (2018: 8). When patriarchalism is perceived as a 'hostile' (man-hating) ideology, then hostility accrues to the feminist who uses it. Typically, it was the radical feminist to whom the image of the man-hating woman was ascribed.

Like all the feminisms, radical feminism has a complex history core to which is the tension between the embrace of a pro-woman culture and a separatist withdrawal from the heterosexual matrix. Anna Coote and Beatrix Campbell explain that while radical feminists in the seventies were able to get behind the idea 'that the fight for women's liberation [was] primarily *against* men', they differed as to what form the struggle should take (1982: 29). One strain of British radical feminism posited separatism as a 'strategic necessity rather than a political goal', arguing a stance that claimed to be 'not anti-man but pro-woman' (ibid.). This differed from the position taken by radical feminists who viewed separatism as a 'political goal'. Notably, it was the Leeds Revolutionary Group who in 1979 declared 'We do think all feminists can and should be political lesbians' (ibid.: 30–31), a position that cemented radical feminism with political lesbianism. The tensions between these different stances were a matter of debate among radical and socialist feminists. This was not least because in reality political positions and sexualities were far more fluid: 'A considerable number of heterosexuals have espoused the radical feminist cause, while many lesbians are committed socialist feminists' (ibid.: 31). It is important to note this degree of fluidity: despite the tensions within radical feminism and between radical and socialist feminisms, going forward there were synergies that helped overcome some of these feminist-political divides. Significantly, the concept of patriarchy understood as 'the combination of social, economic and cultural systems which ensures male supremacy' (ibid.: 32) was one idea that generated broad feminist agreement. Socialist feminists were drawn more to women's class-based, economic subordination within a patriarchal and capitalist system (see Chapter 4), but that did not detract from a radical-feminist emphasis on the patriarchalism that underpinned male violence against women. Brought together, these different emphases from either side of the socialist- and radical-feminist divides, gestured to a shared interest in combating 'male supremacy'.

However, such synergies did not translate into a loss of distinctiveness between the feminisms. In her assessment of the key features that help to distinguish radical feminism from other feminisms, Finn Mackay proposes four elements that define the radical-feminist terrain: a belief in patriarchy and the need to end it; advocacy of 'women-only space and women-only political organising'; recognition of 'male violence against women as a keystone of women's oppression'; and an acknowledgement of 'male violence against women' that extends to the analysis of 'institutions of pornography and prostitution' (2015: 61). Above all, she makes the indisputable claim that '[i]t was radical feminism which arguably wrote the book on what male violence against women is, why it happens and what we can do to end it' (ibid.: 55).

Looking back at the histories and theories of radical feminism and declaring her own radical-feminist position among the feminisms she surveys, Mackay observes that 'there has not been much support for radical or revolutionary feminism thus far' (2015: 59). That said, if, when compared to the radical and revolutionary feminisms of the seventies, women today appear less inclined to identify *as* radical feminists, women's identification *with* the radical-feminist goal to end patriarchalism has garnered significant 'support'. As Chantal Mouffe observes, the 'struggles against sexism' which 'have become increasingly central' to the fight for democracy constitute an important link in the 'chain of equivalence among the manifold struggles against subordination' (2018: 6). And behind the 'struggles against sexism' stands the knowledge of patriarchalism produced by radical-feminist thinking and activism—an understanding beneficial to the widely felt realisation among diverse constituencies of women that patriarchy must end.

'Me Too': Speaking Disobedience and Thinking Towards Ideas-Affections

An end to patriarchy that sanctions the male abuse of power is what each woman demanded when, post-Weinstein, she displayed #Me Too on her social media, thereby reigniting the 'Me Too' Movement founded by Black American activist, Tarana Burke in 2006. Summarising the backlash against #Me Too conducted in the media—the complaint that it has 'gone too far' and men are being wrongly accused, that it does not distinguish between major or minor transgressions, or that women might be complicit in condoning sexism to advance their careers—Kennedy persuasively argues that ultimately what the movement signifies is 'women having had enough and actually refusing to be victims': 'a form of civil disobedience and it should be seen as an alarm call' (2018: 11). I fully concur with Kennedy's observations, but also want to unpack the idea of #Me Too as disobedient speech endowed with a capacity to ignite attachments to anti-patriarchal sentiments.

In his highly illuminating essay 'On the Performance of "Dissensual Speech"', Tony Fisher analyses the phatic and agonic dimensions to speaking dissent. As a phatic utterance, 'me too' obeys the 'logic' of equivalence that characterises the phatic mode in which 'the parity of speakers' is 'constitutive of the speech situation' (Fisher 2017: 200). It is the phatic mode in which it 'becomes possible for one speaker to call across the immemorial silence of inert and dumb matter to another subject in mutual recognition: an "I" who speaks "here" and invites the response of the "I" that is always already "there" in solidarity and understanding' (ibid.: 201). By this means, phatic communication verifies what speakers have in 'common' before 'the rule of authorised speech' that regulates social relations, hierarchies and inequalities (ibid.). The phatic 'me too' establishes that what the speakers have in 'common' is the injustice of an abusive system of masculinist power. Thus, where the phatic mode is generally the preserve of inconsequential small talk, it is 'the element of a grievance' (ibid.) that serves to radicalise it. Since it is agonic speech that 'brings the political community of the people whoever they may be, into existence under the sign of the injustice done to it' (ibid.), we can understand the phatic *and* agonic modes of 'me too' as bringing 'into existence' a 'political community' resistant to the hegemonic formation of patriarchal power.

But there is a further element to consider besides the phatic and the agonic and that is the affective dimension. On the one hand, speaking disobedience 'me too' utters the gender injustice that patriarchalism dictates should not be heard and thereby enunciates the non-performative (broken) promise of women's emancipation. On the other, it repeats ad infinitum the *ressentiment* against male abuses of power and implicit in that hostility is the desire for women's emancipation. In other words, the phatic/agonic contestation of patriarchy is motivated by *feelings* of injustice and the *longing* for a more equitable social order. Unlike the individualistic 'I' who believes she has the freedom to choose, the woman who identifies with #Me Too realises the power of patriarchy to injure. As the feeling-voicing of injury multiplies, the woman who declares 'me too' becomes one of the many—a disobedient, collectivist subject who dissents from the unspoken 'law' of male supremacy.

Hence, as affectively rendered dissensual speech, #Me Too attests to what Mouffe describes as the importance of affect in the formation of political attachments. In her analysis of collective modes of identification, she returns to Spinoza's distinction between affections and affects positing affections as 'the practices where the discursive and the affective are articulated, producing specific forms of identification' (2018: 74). To elaborate: Spinoza's 'ideas of affections' are the 'images of things' by which we are affected; the 'affections' or 'modes' formed by 'external causes' that affect our 'desire' to act in one way or another (Spinoza 1996: 47, 87). Following Mouffe's Spinozan-derived claims to the artistic 'production of ideas with the power to affect' (2018: 75), my performance analysis of *The Suppliant Women* in this chapter pivots around the creation of those ideas-affections which, like #Me Too, mobilise anti-patriarchal, radical-feminist sentiments.

Furthermore, in Spinoza's thinking our 'striving' to exist, to 'persevere in [our] being', means that we are '*opposed to everything which can take [our] existence away*' (ibid.: 75; emphasis added); we need to oppose 'everything' which decreases our 'power of acting' (ibid.: 78). Hence, a feminist imagination necessitates striving for the production of ideas-affections which increase women's 'power of acting'. By this, I do not intend the neoliberal sense of individualistic empowerment, but a collectivist, social-democratic mode of imagining and 'acting' in the interests of all women. Thus, in my second case study of Malcolm's *Emilia*, alongside tracing radical-feminist objections to patriarchalism which diminishes women's 'power of acting', I reflect on how the show ultimately strives to imagine the feminist-political power of a diverse body of women 'acting' together.

Supplication and Demonstration: *The Suppliant Women*

From her radical-feminist perspective, Mackay defines 'the project of feminism' as 'deconstructing male power', where 'male power' is understood as a 'social structure' whose production of gender inequality demands a 'political response' (2015: 127). In a similar vein, Mary Beard insists that '[y]ou cannot easily fit women into a structure that is already coded as male; you have to change the structure' (2017: 86–87). Changing the structure of 'male power' is an urgent and necessary, yet also daunting feminist project: patriarchy may have shapeshifted over centuries, but it has repeatedly and relentlessly served to structure gender inequality. Beard advises that in the interests of moving beyond 'the simple diagnosis of "misogyny"' and thinking towards the transformation of 'male power', one place to begin is with the 'long back-story': to go back to the classical world as a point of departure (ibid.: 8).

I admit that returning to the classics does not come easily to me: in the pioneering phase of feminism and theatre, the recognition of women's absence from classical stages was paramount. 'Deconstructing the male power' of classical plays from antiquity or the Elizabethan stage and their modes of all-male performance, involved understanding how these functioned as 'allies in the project of suppressing real women and replacing them with the masks of patriarchal production' (Case 2008 [1988]: 7). Nonetheless, as Sue-Ellen Case concluded in her analysis of Greek drama and the discomfort for the feminist reader produced by her encounter with the 'male-identified woman', the unmasking of patriarchalism was instructive in 'understanding how the hegemonic structure of patriarchal practice was instituted in Athens', on and off the stage (ibid.: 15). Contemporary revivals of ancient drama might comparably elicit understandings of patriarchal power, past and present, that are beneficial to the project of deconstructing and changing it.

What initially drew me to Greig's restaging of *The Suppliant Women* was the online publicity about the production's female chorus: the intention was to form a community chorus alongside professional actors, a chorus that overturned the ancient, male-only acting tradition by involving the participation of 30 or more young women (between the ages of

16 and 26) from the city of Edinburgh. My interest also was piqued by knowing that in Aeschylus' tragedy it is the chorus who appears as the main protagonist. The chorus of suppliant women are the catalyst for the drama which hinges on whether the Greek city of Argos will grant them asylum from enforced marriage and the threat of male violence in the East (Egypt). The dilemma for King Pelasgos and the citizens of Argos is whether to grant the women sanctuary when this will invite war on the city, a dilemma that is resolved by putting the women's plight to a democratic vote. Hence, there was highly contemporary feeling to the play's subject matter: the democratic process of voting evocative of the Scottish Independence Referendum in 2014 and the Brexit Referendum of 2016; the urgent question of sanctuary produced by the Syrian refugee crisis of 2015 (Syria is named by Aeschylus in the chorus's opening stanza); and, not least, the question of women's rights.

The production history of *The Suppliant Women* dates from October 2016 when Greig, Scotland's foremost contemporary playwright, took up the post of Artistic Director of Edinburgh's Royal Lyceum Theatre and opened his inaugural season with his new version of Aeschylus' tragedy. It was staged in a co-production with the Actors Touring Company (ATC), directed by Ramin Gray. The idea for the community chorus was seeded by an earlier collaboration between Greig and Gray: in 2013 ATC staged Greig's *The Events*—a play inspired by the 2011 terrorist attacks in Norway by Anders Behring Breivik. Looking to theatre as a space in which to engage with how to come to terms with an unthinkable event like the attacks in Norway, Greig conceived *The Events* as a drama with two professional acting roles to be accompanied by amateur, local choirs whose function, like that of a Greek chorus, was to bear witness to and struggle to come to terms with tragic events that surpass comprehension. Where *The Events* deployed established choirs that changed from performance to performance, *The Suppliant Women* required a more sustained level of engagement from the chorus of young Edinburgh women; they were engaged for a six-week period of rehearsal time. Greig and Gray considered the volunteer chorus a way to reassess 'the terms of engagement between professional theatre, and the community to which it is supposed to speak' (McMillan 2016). For Greig especially as the incoming Artistic Director of the Lyceum, this presented a moment to signpost his vision for the theatre: democratising the stage for the citizens of Edinburgh through increased modes of participation—an objective highly resonant with Mouffe's claim that 'traditional forms of art' and the institutions that house them do not necessarily conform to conservatism and might be used for democratic ends (2013: 99). That said, in an industry in which inequalities are widespread and highly manifest (as outlined in Chapter 1), the gendered economic divide between unwaged, female amateur and waged, male professional could not and did not go unremarked (Runcie 2016).

The production left Edinburgh to tour to other cities with new choruses drawn from each city. In 2016, it went to Belfast in Northern Ireland and Newcastle in the North East. In 2017, it was staged in the round at Manchester's Royal Exchange Theatre; I went back for a repeat viewing and came away with a reinvigorated impression of the chorus. Seated at ground level in proximity to the chorus whose choreographies of petitioning against male violence circled the playing space, heightened the viscerality of their supplication. From Manchester, the production went to the Dublin Theatre Festival and then in November to the Young Vic, London, by which point its reception was framed by the Weinstein effect. As critic Susannah Clapp observed, at the start of the run the production 'must then have seemed a terrible chronicle of people forced from their homes', but '[g]iven the events of recent weeks this now appears incontestably as a play about women in the power of, and sexually oppressed by, men' (2017). This was not least due to allegations of harassment brought against the show's director, Gray. In an online interview with Carl Woodward, Gray had declared 'I think the search for who is the Weinstein of British theatre is an honourable search and some names have come up. More may come up. It is a terribly traumatic process and it's right that we are examining it and bringing stuff to light' (qtd. in Woodward 2017). Because of that statement, eight women came forward to make allegations of historic harassment against Gray (Wiegand 2017).

Were London's theatre critics to boycott the press night as a form of protest? The issue was aired at length by Maddy Costa in the *Exeunt Magazine*. Costa did attend and reviewed the production, publishing tweets by theatre blogger Megan Vaughan calling for a boycott alongside her own justification for deciding to review the show: questioning the 'solidarity of silence' as an effective action and advocating her professional role as beneficial to 'scrutinising the context' (Costa 2017). Although Costa found much to admire in the work of the chorus and their 'muscular musicality', she was also critical about the choice of a Greek drama: 'A culture is shaped by the stories repeatedly told and retold, and the use of women as a mouthpiece – however laudable, however exhilarating – doesn't make any more palatable the inevitability of the stories that stick' (ibid.). 'One of the results', of men 'maintain[ing] the cultural currency of this 2500-year-old play', she protested, is the 'limiting of space for the storytelling of women' (ibid.). This is an important feminist issue: not enough women playwrights breaking through the industry's glass ceiling; not enough stories by women acquiring cultural 'stickiness', or moving women centre stage, as per the Sphinx Test, to decentre the canonical tradition of the male-dominated narrative (see Chapter 1).[1] Of course, one of the frequently made claims about Greek drama, as Stephen Wilmer describes, is that for contemporary directors and playwrights it affords a source of 'strong female characters [...] who can speak to the current generation about the condition of women and the potential for women to be active in shaping their present and their future' (2005: xiv). But is it not still problematic, Costa persists, if the timeliness of a production like *The Suppliant Women* 'belies its timelessness': when it merely restages 'the universal structure of patriarchy [that] has repeatedly, over millennia, successfully dismissed its challenge' (2017)? Again, this is a legitimate worry and one that I share. And yet, to dismiss the production is to overlook how the formation of a dialectical relationship between the moving (in all senses) chorus of contemporary women and the canonical text serves to articulate a renewed radical-feminist demand to end a patriarchal culture, on and off the stage. Hence, in what follows, I analyse the show's ideas-affections that critique and 'challenge' patriarchalism's 'long backstory'—ideas-affections rendered by the 'muscular musicality' of the community chorus in combination with Greig's demotic-poetic rendition of the tragedy.

The production opens with a tongue-in-cheek libation ceremony, after which the lights dim and the chorus assemble at the back of the Lyceum stage.[2] Carrying the suppliant branches wound in strips of white cloth in their left hands and with heads bent, the women chant their arrival in Argos, moving forward in a rhythmic, foot-pounding formation. They are all in contemporary dress: there is no attempt to costume them in some sort of ancient garb, nor to find a uniform alternative, although they do all shoulder black scarves. Neither do they choreographically produce a chorus-line of idealised femininity and perfect, perfected movements. That is not to say that the choreography directed by Sasha Milavic Davies and guided in performance by Gemma May was of poor quality. Rather, it was the undisguised everydayness of the women and the rough edges to their collective stamping, chanting, singing and waving of branches that I experienced as visceral and energising as they announced their asylum-seeking arrival on the shores of Argos. Speaking as one, they protest the 'hawk-like men' chasing them across the seas; the 'ship full of rape', the 'ship full of man-imals, hunting for girl-flesh' (Greig 2017: 12, 13). Furthermore, the protesting energies of the women's tribal assembly were resonant in Lizzie Clachan's set. Instead of conjuring up the idea of a temple as a place of asylum and sanctuary, her design denoted the outdoor public space of the agora—the square where many of today's dramas of political protest are acted out. Evocative of 'movements of the squares' (Mouffe 2018: 19), the young women's tribal occupation of the stage counterpoints their vulnerable, petitioning status.

Thus, my first impressions of the chorus were of a moving body of assertive women, vociferous in their objection to male violence and determined on the right to sanctuary, so resolute that their father, Danaos (Omar Ebrahim) counsels: 'Be demure, keep your eyes low, always be modest' (Greig 2017: 16). The chorus receive this counsel in a crouched formation, their gaze directed outwards to the auditorium implicating us (the audience) in the decision-making process. When the city's King arrives (Oscar Batterham) besuited and business-like, his first impression is of 'strange women', 'brazen' in their occupation of the temple (ibid.: 18). Since they are unaccompanied by men, he wonders whether they hail from a matriarchal tribe; if they 'had spears', then he would suspect they 'were Amazon warrior queens/ With no husbands' (ibid.: 19). A threatened and threatening (castrating) presence, the chorus claim Greek citizenship based on matrilineal descent from Io and declare that they are not militaristic, but 'women in fear' (ibid.: 22). Hence, diasporic belonging to Argos is invoked alongside the universal right of all women to live without 'fear' of male violence. Claiming that right shifts the question of who they are to the 'who-ness' of the city: Is this a city whose democratic order is bordered and closed, or open and receptive to their petition?

Their petitioning mobilises the political wheel around which the drama turns. The King faces an agonising decision: To protect the city and sanction the tyranny of rape, or protect the women and risk bringing war to the city? The idea-affection of conflicting political interests is rendered as the women encircle Pelasgos with their bodies and sticks, urge his support even while he demands time to think. As Stephe Harrop describes in her excellent analysis of the production's exemplification of 'agonistic spatial practice', the chorus 'press their case by spatial means', 'driving the king downstage until he is pressed back against the extreme edge of the thrust stage', thereby 'intensifying the sense that Aeschylus' tragic dramaturgy hinges on the uneasy spatial and political co-presence of two opposed groups within a single polity' (2018: 106). As Harrop further observes, the agonistic 'dramaturgy' of the stage relates to that of Athenian politics; she draws highly insightful connections between Mouffe's agonistic framework and the agonic characteristics of Greek theatre and the polis. To which I would add that the women's agonistic petitioning and occupation of the stage structures a feeling of today's neoliberal 'polity' and its patriarchal shortcomings. Only a political regime versed in the language of democracy has the capacity to mobilise the 'will of the people' to 'stand up for women', 'stand against rape' (Greig 2017: 24, 32).

If the King refuses to assist them, the women have vowed to commit mass suicide in the temple and bring 'shame' on the city 'forever' (ibid.: 26). Speaking as exilic women, the suppliants have no power or authority. To speak without authority against oppression carries a risk, exemplified by their commissive utterance 'We'll hang ourselves' (ibid.: 15), a line delivered in unison with a stress on and pause between each word, that binds them to taking their own lives. As Fisher points out, commissives within unauthorised, dissensual speech entail a risk to the speaker (2017: 202). He elaborates that in the interests of democracy, a shared risk can be evidenced in the 'commissive that communises': one that 'embodies the paradox of becoming a singular-plural subject' as not one but several speakers bind themselves to a 'commitment in the name of collective or general equality' (ibid.: 204). As a 'singular-plural subject' uttering their 'communising' commissive 'We'll hang ourselves', the chorus of suppliants commits not one woman to acting alone on behalf of the others but binds all women to act in solidarity—to choose death over social death under a regime of male violence.

Two women-only rituals are performed in the wake of the petitioning. The first is an exultation of the suppliants' matrilineal descent from Io who was forced by the goddess Hera to take the form of a cow.[3] Adjourning to await the outcome of the city's vote, the chorus create the idea-affection of a women-only space as restorative and celebratory: they lay down their black scarves to map out the silhouette of a cow on the stage floor; proclaim Greek and bovine kinship; and spill white liquid in a ritualised birthing sequence of the child Io bore Zeus on the banks of the Nile. The eco-feminist dimension enveloped in this visually arresting, collective image-making advocated the coexistence of human and non-human life forms thereby lending weight to the women's supplication as a plea to protect not only their lives but *all* forms of life.

Where this ritual is restorative, the second consists of a vigil which remarks the women's precarity. After being granted leave to remain and singing their joyful thanks while confetti streams down on to the stage, the suppliants learn that the Egyptians are coming to reclaim them. Thus, the women keep night-time watch in the temple and cover their heads in the black scarves and, exceptionally, the unity of voices chanting as one fracture into individually spoken lines. Instead of the 'we' it is the 'I' who speaks of being 'broken' and 'exhausted' (Greig 2017: 36). As each suppliant collected a candle in a jam jar from the chorus leader to populate the darkened stage with flickering flames, in both the Edinburgh and Manchester performances I was struck by the resonance of the radical-feminist vigil: women's peaceful-protest tradition of reclaiming the night from male violence. The vigil is violently disrupted by the arrival of the chorus of Egyptian men who bear flaming torches that dwarf the women's candles; they chant their aggressive intention to take the women by 'force': 'Come to meet our fists, your masters' (ibid.: 39). Fearful but nonetheless resistant, the women jointly curse the 'Maggoty-meat men/Rats-in-a-drain men' (ibid.: 40) until the King reappears to claim them under his paternalistic protection.

That the women's survival necessarily depends on patriarchal protection raises the issue of protectionism. The idea of protection in the form of patriarchal surveillance is rendered as Danaos/Ebrahim lectures the chorus on how they must adapt to living their lives as chaste, subordinate, migrant women in the Greek city.[4] Thus, as Judith Butler asks, under conditions of precarity where state support for survival is required, how are we to make 'the feminist claim' that such support is necessary 'to sustaining lives' and 'at the same time [...] resist modes of paternalism that reinstate and naturalize relations of inequality' (2015: 142)? How to recognise the legitimacy of feminism's long-standing and rightful claim to the way in which 'women suffer social vulnerability disproportionately', when this risks women being defined by their 'vulnerability' and requiring 'paternalistic provisions of protection' (ibid.: 140)? Butler proposes coupling 'vulnerability and resistance' to advocate that 'women are at once vulnerable and capable of resistance' (ibid.: 141). To that end, she distinguishes between feminism activated in a judicial context and feminist claims voiced in 'popular and extralegal contexts' (ibid.: 142). In the former, to appeal women's rights and protection there is a need to stress vulnerability; in the latter, vulnerability is mobilised 'as a deliberate and active form of political resistance, an exposure of the body to power in the plural action of resistance' (ibid.: 184).

Overall, *The Suppliant Women* puts both contexts into play: interweaves supplication (judicial petitioning) and demonstration (popular protest). Where the suppliants' petitioning of Argos to legislate for their right to remain is driven by the dramatic action of the tragedy, the protest-like occupation of the stage by the young Edinburgh women is enacted through their dissensual 'speech' embodied in the collective chanting, vigorous feet stamping, noisy handclapping, sinewy swirling and choric circling, or archaic cries of anger. Thus, dramaturgies of protest and petition combine to suggest both are necessary to deepen democracy: to mobilise the 'will of the people' to end male violence against women takes popular protest *and* political *and* legal processes. Where protest signifies an antagonism towards the state, ultimately an agonistic engagement *with* rather than withdrawal from the state is necessary if women's universal right to freedom from male violence is to be heard, legislated for and acted upon.[5]

The play ends with a sense of the women's agonistic struggle with the state as ongoing rather than concluded. The suppliants are welcomed into the city of Argos represented by another volunteer chorus of a dozen or so older women, dressed in black and carrying white lilies. The female elders of Argos counsel marriage as preferable to war, but the young women voice an outright rejection of matrimony. They are 'wedded' to another 'communising' commissive: 'we'll never have men' (Greig 2017: 45). Hence, a radical-feminist voicing of separatism augers an imminent disturbance of women's conventional, heterosexually configured role in the Greek city.

Disobedient and defiant, strident and tribal, the women collectively draw breath to deliver their final note of feminist protest: 'Give equal power to all women'.[6] 'Equal power to do what exactly?' complained Costa who found this 'extraordinary moment, galvanising, utterly convincing – and utterly flawed' (2017). To increase women's socially democratic power of acting together to end an injurious patriarchalism is my response, an idea-affection that moves centre stage in my second case study, *Emilia*.

'Muscle Memory' of Radical-Feminist Rage: *Emilia*

Where my other case-study choices were informed by prior knowledge and expectations of what each production might yield regarding the idea of restaging feminisms, *Emilia* was an unexpected discovery. The playwright Morgan Lloyd Malcolm was not on my feminist-theatre radar; historically themed new dramas are not what I would normally seek out; and there were my reservations about a canonical, Shakespearean culture, even though a cursory glance at the publicity alerted me to the promise of a feminist intervention into the life and Shakespearean times of the poet Emilia Bassano. So, imagine my joy when *Emilia* turned out to be an exuberant and passionate voicing of radical feminism. It is never easy 'to pin down any feeling of joy', writes Lynne Segal, 'seeing how easily pleasure mixes with sorrow', but 'what is most distinctive about moments of joy is that, tending to arrive unexpectedly, they raise us altogether above our routine concerns' (2017: 44). The unexpected, joyous discovery of *Emilia* during my academic 'routine' of researching and writing this book is what lead to its inclusion in this chapter.

The play itself produces an uneasy mix of 'pleasure' and 'sorrow': the joy that derives from the power of women acting together and women's power of acting diminished by patriarchy. Spinoza posits three 'primitive' or primary affects to which all other affects are related: joy, sadness and desire (1996: 101). Of the three, desire is identified as constituting our determination 'to do something'; a desire to 'act' is shaped by 'external causes' that give rise to the 'passions' of joy or sadness in accordance with how a desire is positively or adversely affected (ibid.: 100). In its writing and staging, the desire for women's stories to move centre stage drives the action of *Emilia*; joy and sadness oscillate as Emilia Bassano (1569–1645), a woman determined to write and see her poetry in print, struggles against the patriarchalism of her time that is also, Malcolm makes clear, our time. The play's triangulation of desire, joy and sadness will inform my analysis of the show's radical-feminist dynamics, but first I need to outline the background to the production. Given my uninformed discovery and unanticipated pleasure of *Emilia*, these are details which I pieced together after the event.

What I discovered about Malcolm's writing career is that it exemplifies the difficulty of getting established as a playwright and pursuing a writing profession without substantial means—hardships that increased after the birth of her two children and the juggling of theatrical labour with maternal labour. Briefly, she began her career by collaborating with women on comedic pieces for the Edinburgh fringe; participated in the inaugural year of the Old Vic's 'New Voices' scheme (2005); worked on community shows; and found employment team-scripting pantomimes at the Lyric Hammersmith (Malcolm 2019b). Whatever theatre work she took on was subsidised by other jobs, a characteristic of the industry that Malcolm insists needs to change: 'We've managed to get other jobs to cover the fact we're not being paid very well by what we are doing within the industry. It's interesting that that's just an accepted part of our jobs, and I don't think it's right. Particularly when it comes to things like childcare' (ibid.; see also related discussion in Chapter 1). It was only through an attachment to the National Theatre that Malcolm was finally able to write her first full-length play, *Belongings*—a drama staged at the Hampstead Theatre (2011). The Hampstead subsequently premiered her female, two-hander *The Wasp* (2015) that transferred to the West End Trafalgar Studios.

The idea for *Emilia* originally came from actress Michelle Terry who in 2017 was appointed Artistic Director of the Globe Theatre in the wake of Emma Rice's controversial departure from the position after just two seasons. Formerly Artistic Director of the internationally acclaimed Kneehigh company, Rice resigned from the Globe over her exclusion from decisions made in the theatre's executive boardroom that she deemed likely to hinder her creative freedom and experimental approach to Shakespeare (Brown 2016; Gardner 2016). Hence, it was vital that Terry steered the theatre away from controversy; the path she chose was one of democratisation—a redistributive model of ensemble playing, diverse representation and a commitment to a 50/50 gender split across a season (Tripney 2019).

Encouraged and commissioned by Terry, in August 2018 Malcolm brought *Emilia* to the Globe where it received just 11 performances. However, given the play's rapturous reception it was picked up by the West End Vaudeville Theatre and transferred in March 2019 which is where I caught up with the show. Exemplifying Terry and Malcolm's shared commitment to democratising the stage, *Emilia* had an all-female creative team and an ensemble cast of women from diverse ethnicities, different ages and disabilities. From a disabilities point of view, what was distinctive was the 'lack of a specific "disabled narrative" [which] is incredibly rare within productions that sit outside of the disability arts world, and unheard of in a West End show. A revolutionary moment: disabled actors in the West End solely because they are superb performers' (Lovell 2019). Other elements that signified a democratisation of the West End included the absence of star performers and a relatively low budget and ticket prices; I paid £25 for a seat in the stalls some three or four rows back from the stage. Furthermore, the Vaudeville broke new ground by organising a baby-friendly matinee performance, an event promoted as 'Let Them Roar'. For Malcolm, this was an important initiative in encouraging the West End to be a more inclusive sector: 'If we exclude any sector of society from seeing art I think that is a big problem. It's our duty as theatre makers to make sure we change that system' (qtd. in Wiegand 2019).

In her 'note on the text', Malcolm advises that future productions of *Emilia* should recognise that the play 'was written to be performed by an all female cast of diverse women. It would not be the same play if this is ignored' (2018: vii). She also explains that she wrote *Emilia* 'to challenge the notion that a play about a person needs to be a vehicle for one actress' (ibid.). In the biographical re-telling of Emilia's life which forms the narrative arc of the play, Malcolm evokes the feminist-theatre tradition of rendering the biographical subject multiple rather than singular.[7] Three women of colour, of mixed heritage, were cast in the main role: Emilia1 (Saffron Coomber) represents the poet in her youth; Emilia2 (Adelle Leonce) in her middle years; and Emilia3 (Clare Perkins) presents her later life.[8] Jointly configured as the auto/biographical, storytelling I/eye, all three performers wove the biographical layers together, acting out and commenting on life-changing events and the constant patriarchal thwarting of Emilia's desire to write and be published.

All told, the intersectionality which Malcolm conceived as integral and essential to the production signals a significant, progressive shift. As Gerry Harris and I note about the popular-feminist shows we researched for *A Good Night Out for the Girls*, these and their audiences were 'overwhelmingly white' (2013: 158). To quote Coomber, the youngest of the Emilias, 'I think 10 years ago, when I was a teenager, if you had told me about this play — in the West End, all women, and the leads all mixed heritage, about a historical figure who has almost been written out of history — I would not have believed you' (qtd. in Lee 2019).

Furthermore, given how Malcolm advised the cast in rehearsal to think of Emilia's story as an 'every woman's story' (ibid.), diversity was vital to overcoming the idea that an 'every woman's story' means a white 'woman's story'. This is an essential corrective to radical feminism's second-wave, pro-woman's stance where the focus on the commonality of women's experience tended to presume a commonality that was exclusionary (white, straight, middle-class, able-bodied) rather than inclusive. As outlined in Chapter 1, it was the exclusionary tendencies of the feminist movement that occasioned its fragmentation into 'competing political identities' that made it difficult for 'women [to] share some common political interests' (Lovenduski and Randall 1993: 89). Recollecting this fragmentation of the women's movement further attests to Malcolm's inclusive approach to the writing and staging of *Emilia* as a way to restore the idea of 'common political interests': to realise what bell hooks describes as 'identity-based bonding' based on a '*commonality of feeling*', a 'yearning to be in a more *just* world' (1994: 217, original emphasis).

Under Nicole Charles' direction, the show mobilised a 'commonality of feeling' through its popular-feminist treatment of the 'struggles against sexism' that Malcolm imagines characterising Bassano's life and times as well as our present day. Unlike the other plays I have considered thus far which were written before the Weinstein watershed but whose production histories intersected with the #Me Too movement, *Emilia* was written post-Weinstein. Malcolm was conscious of the 'timing'; the play was credited as being the first #Me Too play (Lee 2019). It is interesting to note that the actresses playing Emilia hold agonistic (in Mouffe's sense) views of the parallel between #Me Too and the show. Leonce acknowledges the connection but argues 'you don't come into a project thinking that'; Perkins is more sceptical about whether, despite #Me Too opening up an important 'conversation', it necessarily encourages audiences to 'see a play described like that'; Coomber, contrastingly, enthusiastically endorses #Me Too and the play as mediums that for her generation give 'voice' to 'ancestors' silenced by history (all quotations in Lee 2019). Ultimately, perhaps one way to think of *Emilia* is as a play that, as Leonce puts it, 'really opens up the conversations we have to have' (ibid.).

There is an openness to the form of *Emilia* that stems from the way it was written to be performed at the Globe, a venue that invites a direct and immersive quality in audience-performer relations.[9] Malcolm and the women creatives involved in *Emilia* thought of the play not as an historical drama but a 'Memory Play': an act of remembrance that encourages audiences to think of all the forgotten herstories and potentially to come away feel 'empowered' (Malcolm 2019a). Generically, I find *Emilia* hard to pin down; that is not a criticism but an indication of the play's strength in its exemplification of a feminist unruliness and disobedience—a refusal to be generically faithfully to one monolithic form or another. In its treatment of high culture, the play is carnivalesque; it comically deflates the canonicity accorded to Shakespeare. History is not approached as an epistemological quest for historical facts or truths; instead, the scant details of Bassano's life recorded and passed down through a masculinist imagination[10] are restaged as a feminist imagining of struggles against patriarchalism. And there is a pantomimic, immersive dimension, well-suited to the Globe with its thrust stage and circular yard that allows performers to mix with the groundlings, but also, despite the limitations of the Vaudeville's proscenium arch, still very much in play during the West End production. Hence, summative descriptions from those commentators and critics who warmed to the play (and most did) variously signalled the affective and feminist-political qualities of the production: 'a passionately considered manifesto rather than a cautious history lesson' (Taylor 2018); 'an entertaining, anarchic and revolutionary work that has enormous weight, passion, humour and debate' (Pascal 2018); and 'an inspired and inspiring conjuration of a truly remarkable, ignored and forgotten spirit' (Woddis 2018).

Coming back to my promise to reflect on the constellation of joy, desire and sadness in relation to the play's radical-feminist dynamics, I turn first to joy. It struck me when writing how hard it is to communicate a joyful experience without it turning into a joyless exercise. With that in mind, to keep hold of the joy I felt during and after *Emilia* I made the decision to eschew my customary approach to reviews of a production. As my analysis of the reception of *The Suppliant Women* exemplifies, when analysing a production I normally give weight and counterweight to positive and negative reviews with a view to understanding different perspectives: to analysing how it is that what I see is possibly not what others see, and so forth. In this instance, although I read a raft of reviews and commentaries, I set aside any negative quibbles and arguments over the production and did not pursue them. Equally, a few minutes into listening to a recording of BBC4's *Front Row* slot on *Emilia* (10 August 2018) in which Germaine Greer began to deliver a joyless commentary on whether Emilia was the Dark Lady of Shakespeare's sonnets, I pressed the stop button. Scholarly ruminations of the serious, Shakespearean kind (Greer was invited on to the programme as a Shakespearean scholar, not a feminist) are irrelevant to the production's playful, feminist imagining of Emilia's story in which, moreover, *her* creative inspiration (not Shakespeare's) is paramount (members of the ensemble, clad in white, periodically accompany Emilia as her collective muse). Although my refusal to engage with negative views of the production can justifiably be criticised as a partisan response, I am passionately committed to the idea that now is not the time to kill the joy of an 'anarchic and revolutionary' feminist voicing which urges the case for women's stories to be told on our mainstream stages. Indeed, I feel strongly that the production be regarded as a manifesto for all that the Arts Council promises but has yet to deliver on the equality and diversity front (see Chapter 1).

It is Sara Ahmed who draws attention to the way in which the 'figure of the feminist' is identified as a 'killjoy' (2010: 66). 'Feminists do kill joy in a certain sense', she explains: 'they disturb the very fantasy that happiness can be found in certain places' (ibid.). But her point is 'that feminists are read as being unhappy, such that situations of conflict, violence, and power are read as *about* the unhappiness of feminists, rather than being what feminists are unhappy *about*' (ibid.: 67; original emphasis). Moreover, as I observed in the introduction to this chapter, it is the radical feminist who is particularly regarded as the joyless, unhappy, man-hating woman. But *Emilia's* gendered inversion of the 'killjoy' firmly and resolutely posits patriarchy as that which 'kills' women's desire for equality and by doing so invites a *joyous identification with* radical-feminist dissent from the regulatory power of patriarchalism.

Instead of portraying women as helpless, hapless victims of patriarchy, Malcolm conceives them as, in the words of Emilia's protégé, Lady Anne (Tanika Yearwood) 'shapeshifters and tricksters' (2018: 68). The allusion to the trickster is apposite: as María Lugones points out, this is a figure much celebrated in subordinate, colonised cultures where counter-hegemonic pleasure resides in the idea of the trickster outwitting the coloniser (2003: 92). In Act One, Emilia, an immigrant of Italian descent from a family of court musicians, must learn how to present herself as a lady at the English court; her shapeshifting, slippery behaviour begins with fathoming how to navigate the 'verbal dances' of unwanted male attention (Malcolm 2018: 23). The trick is to appear to conform while inwardly holding heterosexual courtship in contempt. Over the course of the first act, we follow Emilia's life as the mistress of a much older, married man, Lord Henry Carey (patron of Shakespeare's company the Lord Chamberlain's Men); her marriage of convenience to a cousin Alphonso (pregnant by Carey, the marriage is a way of keeping-up appearances); and her sexual attraction to Shakespeare. She births two children: a son who survives and a daughter who dies. In short, she cannot escape convention but learns to dissemble and slip through its cracks.

Accompanying the charade or masquerade of femininity to disguise the 'manly' pursuit of writing is the anarchic-comedic playing of the male parts. A veritable riot of wigs, moustaches, doublets, hoses and ruffs is deployed by the performers in their gender reversal of the all-male, Elizabethan stage. An initial Rabelaisian display of phallic posturing and preening on the part of the lords who dance their attentions on the ladies of the court sets the tone for the production's treatment of masculinity: women (and men) are encouraged to mock and laugh at patriarchy in drag. Just as there are degrees of disobedience among the women characters (some conform, others, like the Emilias, do not), there are shades of buffoonery among the playing of the men, ranging from the affectionately ridiculous, closet gay Alphonso (Amanda Wilkin), through the manly, worldly wise Carey (Carolyn Pickles) to the socially awkward Will Shakespeare (Charity Wakefield). Overall, tricksterish femininities and parodic masculinities combine and conspire to remake and reimagine the Elizabethan world into what, in Ahmed's terms, might be described as a happiness-making object of feminist pleasure.

However, as previously noted the 'primary effect' of joy is not constant but jostles with the negative affect of sadness: specifically, *Emilia* oscillates between the theatrical rendering of ideas-affections which joyously mock patriarchalism and those which elicit sadness at patriarchy's capacity to diminish women's power of acting. The ideas-affections pertaining to the latter escalate through the climactic build to Act One: Emilia, likened by Shakespeare to an 'angry', 'trapped wasp', is stung more than she can sting (Malcolm 2018: 24). Loss of her baby daughter causes grief, but it is not her 'only pain': to live her 'whole existence in [Shakespeare's] shadow' means that her 'own desires' must 'languish in the dark' (ibid.: 35). What Emilia also discovers is that Shakespeare, the object of her sexual desire, has stolen her words, crafted them as his own. This betrayal is revealed as she catches a performance of *Othello* at the Globe Theatre; she arrives in time to hear her words spoken by Shakespeare's Emilia in Act Four of the tragedy. Bassano confronts her on-stage double, taking back her words that admonish men for not acknowledging women also have 'affections, desires for sport and frailty'; letting men 'know, the ills we [women] do, their ills instruct us so' (ibid.: 42). In its staging at the Globe, this metatheatrical episode was commented on as a source of riotous energy as Emilia emerged from among the 'groundlings and stormed the stage' (Malcolm 2019a). Even on the Vaudeville's proscenium stage, the disruption of the Shakespearean spectacle achieved an energising note of feminist protest as Emilia2/Leonce leapt on to the stage to chant at us (the audience) 'The ills we do, their ills instruct us so!' (Malcolm 2018: 42).

The parallel between the power of the 'great' man of theatre (Shakespeare) and the abusive power of the likes of Weinstein is not hard to miss. But the counter-hegemonic pulse of *Emilia* would be significantly reduced if this were to become the primary focus of the show. Stepping away from *Emilia* momentarily to look across at David Mamet's *Bitter Wheat* that opened at the Garrick Theatre in June as Malcolm's show closed, underscores how injurious it is when the idea-affection of the monstrous, powerful, individual man takes centre stage. The misguided and universally panned Weinstein-themed *Bitter Wheat* reverted to the patriarchal set-up of the star tradition with John Malkovich in the role of abusing movie mogul, Barney Fein. I did force myself to see *Bitter Wheat* to ensure that I was not being unduly hostile or dismissive. Or at least I saw part of it: since I refused to pay anything but the minimum, which at £37.50 was still too much, my view was obscured by a pillar. But it was as I suspected: a play that silences, takes back women's voicing of #Me Too by focusing on the atrocious Weinstein figure; in the event the show 'succeeded' purely at the level of re-fuelling my feminist anger against a theatre culture that is not heeding the insistent demand that Malcolm voices through Emilia: 'Time to listen!' to the stories *women* have to tell (Malcolm 2018: 2).[11]

Why is it that there is 'no room at all' for women's stories, wonders Emilia in Act 1 as she walks along Bankside to Shakespeare's 'Wooden O of words': 'We do not ask for them [men] to step aside and go without we merely ask them to let us join. Surely there is enough to go around' (ibid.: 35, 37). Shakespeare refuses to give up power and to help her change 'the rules' by refusing to 'write unless women are also given the same freedoms' (ibid.: 39). Equally, the first act depicts Emilia initially enthralled to Mary Sidney's artistic circle and Sidney's determination to write and publish. But Sidney plays by the competitive rules of individualism and eschews support of other women. Contrastingly, it is in the second act that Emilia comes to realise the alternative, socially progressive possibilities of women acting together in the interests of other women.

Act Two opens with a heightened sense of hilarity as the washerwomen of Bankside sing while they wash and hang up the clothes of their clientele; I can honestly say that in no other performance have I ever had a pair of white long johns wonderfully flown on top of my head! But the mood shifts dramatically as a suicidal Emilia steps into the river Thames. The washerwomen come to her rescue; Emilia gives away her signature blue dress (worn by all three Emilias)[12] and puts on a gown of much poorer cloth to signify a new phase of her life, one in which she will teach the washerwomen how to read and write poetry. Geographically speaking, the washerwomen live in proximity to the realms of courtly entertainment and culture; but their lives are a world apart from the relative wealth and privilege which, even in reduced circumstances, Emilia has been accustomed to. As Lugones attests in her seminal conception of 'world-traveling' across cultural, racial and social differences among women, to move between 'worlds' in a non-hierarchical way calls for a 'loving playfulness' (2003: 95): a suspension of the competitive games conceived by a masculinist imagination; a willingness to be open to and surprised by the 'worlds' of others, playfully inhabiting and reconstructing the 'ground that constructs us as oppressors or as oppressed or as collaborating or colluding with oppression' (ibid.: 96). Travelling to the 'world' of the washerwomen in which striving to exist means dealing with abusive husbands, prostitution and poverty, Emilia is inspired to teach them; but it is they who teach her a loving attitude towards women as they bring her 'into their world' (Malcolm 2018: 63).

With the support of women friends from the 'world' of privilege *and* the 'world' of the washer women, Emilia sets up a scriptorium through which to publish feminist pamphlets. Sitting close to the stage, I found a pamphlet surreptitiously pressed into my hands by one of the washer women; moments later, I was taken by surprise as a 'man' crept beside my aisle seat to snatch the paper away. The visceral sensation of the snatching left me feeling genuinely startled and deprived of the words I had started to read. Amidst all the pantomimic interactions between performers and spectators, this momentary one-on-one interaction was one which for me sensorially amplified the idea of women's voices being violently silenced.

Emilia finally manages to get her poems into print; she writes religious verse encrypted with women-centred messages to get past the censor. But what ought to be a celebratory moment turns to sadness as one of the washerwomen (symbolically named Eve) is burned as a witch for her anti-patriarchal poem published in a pamphlet. The burning of Eve (pyrotechnically enacted on stage) does not extinguish Emilia's desire to write women's herstories: it burns stronger. The penultimate scene between Emilia3 and Shakespeare sees the bard boasting of his stature, proclaiming the theatre as his 'gaff' (ibid.: 73). 'Not right now it isn't', is Emilia3's rejoinder (ibid.).

This feminist reclamation of theatre for the telling of women's stories is underscored in the closing scene as Perkins commands the stage to deliver an astonishing, breath-taking, radical-feminist tirade against the ills of patriarchalism. All the reviews, even the not-quite-so-positive ones, acknowledged the power of her rage-fuelled delivery. In my notes scribbled down immediately after the show I wrote: 'Perkins finds the anger for this speech somewhere deep inside of herself'. Her words reverberated throughout the auditorium as she spoke of the 'muscle memory of every woman who came before me' (ibid.: 74); the burning anger of women whose stories have been ignored for centuries. Quite simply: Perkins ignited a 'commonality of feeling', a widely shared, affective response to the radical-feminist sentiments of the speech, palpable in the way the audience rose to its feet and whooped joyous identification with the notion of 'burn[ing] the whole fucking [patriarchal] house down' (ibid.: 75). If you could not feel it, then likely you were the odd one out.

I know without a shadow of doubt that Perkins' speech will linger in my 'muscle memory' of feminisms restaged in the era of #Me Too. Where before I signalled how hard it is to write about joy without becoming joyless, in closing this chapter I find it just as hard to come back from the passionate voicing and vision of the patriarchal system demolished in the flames of women's anger. So instead of a conventional conclusion, I chose to end with this 'communising' commissive in response to Emila3/Perkins' demand that women 'Don't stop now' (ibid.: 75):

We won't stop now.

Notes

1. Related to this issue, it is worth noting that in programming his second season at the Lyceum Greig moved away from the 'safe options' of canonical Western theatre where '90 per cent' of plays are 'written by white men'; his second season featured more female writers and directors than male (McMillan 2017).
2. Unless otherwise stated production details refer to the Lyceum staging.

3. This was to prevent Io's union with Zeus. Transformed into a cow, Io was persecuted by a gadfly; she fled from country to country, eventually residing in Egypt, and was restored to human form to deliver a child fathered by Zeus.
4. Parenthetically, it is also worth noting that Ebrahim doubled as the women's father and the Egyptian Herald leading the chorus of 'maggoty-meat men', thus representing both sides of the patriarchal coin around which the women spin.
5. This accords with Mouffe's view that social movements play an important role in acting for change, but also need 'to engage with political institutions' (2018: 20).
6. In the published text, the line is 'Give equal power to women' (Greig 2017: 47), but in performance it was chanted as 'Give equal power to *all* women'.
7. For details of former biographical practices in feminist theatre, see my chapter 'Re-figuring Lives' in Aston (1999: 159–170).
8. In the Globe production, Emilia1 was played by Leah Harvey and Emilia2 by Vinette Robinson; Clare Perkins took the part of Emilia3 in both productions.
9. Joanna Scotcher's set for the Vaudeville stage encompassed a semi-circular, scaffolded structure evocative of the Globe's architectural design.
10. Malcolm notes that historians 'had formed an opinion on [Bassano] based on the writings of Simon Forman, who she visited as her astrologer and a kind of counsellor' (2018: 76). Thus, Forman's misogynist portrait comes to frame her work. Malcolm publishes a selection of Bassano's poetry with the playscript to reinforce a feminist lens.
11. My anger also was fuelled by learning that the last two weeks of *Emilia*'s run at the Vaudeville were cancelled for reasons that are unclear, but likely economic. On the other hand, a film adaptation of the play appears to be in the offing.
12. The colour coding of costuming designated red for Emilia's adversaries; blue for her supporters.

Works Cited

Ahmed, S. 2010. *The Promise of Happiness*. Durham: Duke University Press.

Aston, E. 1999. *Feminist Theatre Practice: A Handbook*. London: Routledge.

Aston, E., and G. Harris. 2013. *A Good Night Out for the Girls*. Basingstoke: Palgrave Macmillan.

Bates, L. 2014. *Everyday Sexism*. London: Simon & Schuster.

Beard, M. 2017. *Women and Power: A Manifesto*. London: Profile Books.

Brown, M. 2016. Emma Rice to Step Down as Artistic Director at Shakespeare's Globe. *Guardian*, 25 October. https://www.theguardian.com/stage/2016/oct/25/emma-rice-step-down-artistic-director-shakespeares-globe.

Butler, J. 2015. *Notes Toward a Performative Theory of Assembly*. Cambridge, MA: Harvard University Press.

Case, S. 2008 [1988]. *Feminism and Theatre*. Basingstoke: Palgrave Macmillan.

Clapp, S. 2017. Review of *The Suppliant Women*. *Guardian*, 26 November. https://www.theguardian.com/stage/2017/nov/26/the-suppliant-women-review-young-vic-aeschylus-david-greig.

Coote, A., and B. Campbell. 1982. *Sweet Freedom: The Struggle for Women's Liberation*. London: Picador.

Costa, M. 2017. Review of *The Suppliant Women*. *Exeunt Magazine*, 20 November. http://exeuntmagazine.com/reviews/the-suppliant-women-at-the-young-vic/.

Fisher, T. 2017. On the Performance of 'Dissensual Speech'. In *Performing Antagonism: Theatre, Performance and Radical Democracy*, ed. T. Fisher and E. Katsouraki, 187–207. London: Palgrave Macmillan.

Gardner, L. 2016. Emma Rice Is Right to Experiment at the Globe—Art Should Reinvent Not Replicate. *Guardian*, 28 September. https://www.theguardian.com/stage/theatreblog/2016/sep/28/emma-rice-shakespeares-globe-theatre-modern-audiences.

Greig, D. 2017. *Aeschylus: The Suppliant Women*. London: Faber & Faber.

Harrop, S. 2018. Greek Tragedy, Agonistic Space, and Contemporary Performance. *New Theatre Quarterly* 34 (2): 99–114.

hooks, b. 1994. *Outlaw Culture: Resisting Representations*. London: Routledge.

Kennedy, H. 2018. *Eve Was Shamed: How British Justice Is Failing Women*. London: Chatto & Windus.

Lee, V. 2019. *Emilia* Is Every Woman's Story—It's a Shared Experience. Interview with Saffron Coomber, Clare Perkins and Adelle Leonce. *Evening Standard*, 11 March. https://www.standard.co.uk/go/london/theatre/emilia-interview-saffron-coomber-adelle-leonce-clare-perkins-a4088091.html.

Lovell, K. 2019. Emilia—A West End Show Which Delivers on Diversity. *Disability Arts Online*, 23 April. https://disabilityarts.online/magazine/opinion/emilia-a-west-end-show-which-delivers-on-diversity/.

Lovenduski, J., and V. Randall. 1993. *Contemporary Feminist Politics: Women and Power in Britain*. Oxford: Oxford University Press.

Lugones, M. 2003. *Pilgrimages/Peregrinajes: Theorizing Coalition Against Multiple Oppressions*. Lanham, MD: Rowman & Littlefield.

Mackay, F. 2015. *Radical Feminism: Feminist Activism in Movement*. Basingstoke: Palgrave Macmillan.

Malcolm, M.L. 2018. *Emilia*. London: Oberon.

———. 2019a. A Glimpse Inside with Morgan Lloyd Malcolm-Part 1. *View from the Outside*, 8 March. https://viewfromtheoutside.blog/2019/03/08/a-glimpse-inside-with-morgan-lloyd-malcolm-part-1/.

———. 2019b. A Glimpse Inside with Morgan Lloyd Malcolm-Part 2. *View from the Outside*, 10 March. https://viewfromtheoutside.blog/2019/03/10/a-glimpse-inside-with-morgan-lloyd-malcolm-part-2/.

McMillan, J. 2016. Preview of *The Suppliant Women*. *Scotsman*, 27 September. http://www.scotsman.com/lifestyle/culture/theatre/preview-the-suppliant-women-at-the-royal-lyceum-1-4241294.

———. 2017. Interview with David Greig. *Scotsman*, 9 May. https://www.scotsman.com/arts-and-culture/theatre/theatre-interview-artistic-director-david-greig-talks-about-bringing-greater-diversity-to-the-royal-lyceum-s-programme-for-2017-18-1-4436329.

McRobbie, A. 2009. *The Aftermath of Feminism: Gender, Culture and Social Change*. London: Sage.

Mouffe, C. 2013. *Agonistics: Thinking the World Politically*. London: Verso.

———. 2018. *For a Left Populism*. London: Verso.

Pascal, J. 2018. Review of *Emilia*. August. https://londongrip.co.uk/2018/08/emilia-shakespeares-globe-review-by-julia-pascal/.

Runcie, C. 2016. Review of *The Suppliant Women*. *Telegraph*, 13 October. https://www.telegraph.co.uk/theatre/what-to-see/the-suppliant-women-is-a-powerfully-feminist-timely-comment-on-t/.

Segal, L. 2017. *Radical Happiness: Moments of Collective Joy*. London: Verso.

Spinoza, B. 1996. *Ethics*, trans. Edwin Curley. London: Penguin.

Taylor, P. 2018. Review of *Emilia*. *Independent*, 16 August. https://www.independent.co.uk/arts-entertainment/theatre-dance/reviews/emilia-shakespeares-globe-london-review-landmark-moment-for-the-globe-a8494911.html.

Tripney, N. 2019. Michelle Terry: 'This Job Has Taught Me That Democracy Is Really Hard'. *The Stage*, 29 May. https://www.thestage.co.uk/features/interviews/2019/michelle-terry-this-job-has-taught-me-that-democracy-is-really-hard/.

Walter, N. 2015 [2010]. *Living Dolls: The Return of Sexism*. London: Virago.

Wiegand, C. 2017. Ramin Gray of Actors Touring Company Faces Harassment Allegations. *Guardian*, 20 November. https://www.theguardian.com/stage/2017/nov/20/ramin-gray-actors-touring-company-harassment-allegations.

———. 2019. 'Let Them Roar': West End Stages First Baby-Friendly Performance. *Guardian*, 24 April. https://www.theguardian.com/stage/2019/apr/24/let-them-roar-west-end-stages-first-baby-friendly-performance.

Wilmer, S.E. 2005. Introduction. In *Rebel Women: Staging Ancient Greek Drama Today*, ed. J. Dillon and S.E. Wilmer, xiii–xxv. London: Methuen.

Woddis, C. 2018. Review of *Emilia*. *Woddisreviews*, 18 August. http://woddisreviews.org.uk/reviews/emilia/#more-3781.

Woodward, C. 2017. Interview with Ramin Gray. *Carl Woodward Blog*, 7 November. https://www.mrcarlwoodward.com/interview/atcs-ramin-gray-i-think-the-search-for-who-is-the-weinstein-of-british-theatre-is-an-honourable-search/.

CHAPTER 4

Towards the Great Moving Left Show? Recitals of Socialist Feminism

Abstract Looking back at the vicissitudes of socialist feminism, this chapter revisits socialist-feminist concerns with the inequalities of women's dual labour (domestic and productive). It posits artistic representations of historic struggles by women workers in the fight for justice in the workplace as instructive for contemporary anti-capitalist, socialist-feminist demonstrations of opposition to the economic inequalities of neoliberalism. This argument is rehearsed through a case study of Townsend Theatre's *We Are The Lions Mr Manager*, a popular-political show that commemorates the historic Grunwick strike by Asian women workers in the seventies. Observing the present, political need to acknowledge an ecological dimension to capitalism's exploitation of natural and human resources, the chapter moves to an analysis of playwright Caryl Churchill's eco-socialist feminism in *Escaped Alone* and thereafter concludes with summative remarks on the study as whole.

Keywords Socialist feminism · Anti-capitalism · Grunwick strike · Popular-political theatre · Eco-socialist feminism

On 14 June 2017 national tragedy strikes: Grenfell Tower, a residential block of flats in the London district of North Kensington, is ablaze. It injures lives and takes lives. It destroys homes and leaves survivors traumatised. The days, weeks and months after the fire are a time of mourning but also of social reckoning. The recently completed renovation of the

E. Aston, *Restaging Feminisms*,
https://doi.org/10.1007/978-3-030-40589-2_4

tower with low-cost, highly combustible cladding was a tragedy waiting to happen that need not have happened. 'If "austerity" can sometimes seem a piece of empty political rhetoric, this is its reality', writes social-housing scholar, John Boughton: 'For almost four decades, we have been taught the neoliberal mantra "private good, public bad" and encouraged to see public spending as an evil; ruthless economising as a virtue' (ibid.). Because of that 'mantra': 'We have come to know the price of everything and the value of nothing and have ended with the funeral pyre of Grenfell Tower' (ibid.).

Press and media coverage of the tragedy was extensive; like a tragic-epic Brechtian 'Street Scene' (Brecht 1964: 121), the catastrophe was replayed, retold and debated by victims and firefighters, eyewitnesses and neighbours, politicians and journalists. Currently the subject of an ongoing public enquiry, it is nigh on impossible to avoid the conclusion that Boughton reaches: this social-housing block, its charred remains standing cheek-by-jowl with affluent Kensington properties, evidences a neoliberal Britain abject in its failure to care for the poorer classes. In his poem on Grenfell, Nigerian poet Ben Okri's refrain is: '*If you want to see how the poor die, come see Grenfell Tower*'; he insists and protests it is time 'to look beneath the cladding', the 'Political cladding, Economic cladding, intellectual cladding' (2017; original italics).

As the charred edifice of Grenfell stands as a monument to neoliberalism's monumental disregard for the underprivileged it also testifies to a neoliberalism in crisis: there are too many cracks in its 'political' and 'economic cladding' to be scaffolded. Since the global banking crisis in 2007–2008, the policies of austerity have propped up an ailing economic system to such a spectacularly socially divided extent (i.e. to the benefit of the 1% at the expense of the 99%) that multiple sites of counter-hegemonic resistance have formed to condemn the long-standing foundations of neoliberalism as unstable and unsustainable (see Chapter 1). This 'period of crisis' is one that Chantal Mouffe describes in Gramscian terms as an *interregnum*: a period when 'several tenets of the consensus established around a hegemonic project are challenged', but no solution is yet found (2018: 12). Thus, it constitutes a 'populist moment', one which gives 'expression [to] a variety of resistances to the political and economic transformations seen during the years of neoliberal hegemony' (ibid.). As Mouffe is at pains to point out, such resistances can come from the left *and* the right (ibid.: 5). For a 'left populist strategy' to gain traction, it will need to forge and mobilise a 'chain of equivalence among the manifold struggles against subordination' (ibid.: 6).

Look Back in Socialist-Feminist Anger

As maintained throughout *Restaging Feminisms*, the feminist movement is an important link in the chain of socially progressive struggles. However, historically it was marginalised by the socialist left. When the left was in crisis after the inception of what Stuart Hall termed Margaret Thatcher's 'great moving right show' (1988: 39), it was an anathema to Hall that the left should 'so persistently exclude itself from this [then] new, socially revolutionary force' (ibid.: 249). Thus, there was a contradiction between the relative 'strength of the organized left' that meant 'British feminism' was 'more socialist than its American counterpart' (Coote and Campbell 1982: 31) and the way in which the alignment between the left and feminism was so fraught with antagonisms. Recollecting this misalignment in *Promise of a Dream: Remembering the Sixties*, activist and historian Sheila Rowbotham cites what she experienced as the antipathy of socialist, male comrades towards the notion of 'democratizing daily life' (2019 [2000]: 115): the idea that 'in socialist households men and women shared the housework' (ibid.: 114).[1] In the seventies, the notion of 'democratizing daily life' would prove pivotal to socialist-feminist analysis that extended Marx's idea of class exploitation into a more comprehensive analysis of gender and class subordination. At the intersection of class and gender, it was possible to grasp how working-class women's subordination was structured through a system of capitalist production (work) and social reproduction (home). Over time, socialist-feminist theorising would further extend into interlinkages of class, gender, race and sexuality.[2]

As touched on in Chapter 3, patriarchy was an issue for both radical and socialist feminists. However, whereas the recognition of 'male supremacy' saw radical feminists withdrawing from engagement with men, the socialist-feminist acknowledgement of the 'patriarchal character of economic class relations' occasioned 'an urgent necessity to fight *both in* and *against* male-dominated power relations' (Coote and Campbell 1982: 32–33; original emphasis). Nonetheless, fighting 'in and against' conditions of 'male supremacy' was extremely fatiguing. Thus, for example, Rowbotham recounts how she withdrew from her socialist affiliations to pour her political energies into the Women's Liberation Movement; this was only reversed when the 'election of Margaret Thatcher in 1979 made [her] feel the need to connect back to a wider movement of resistance against the harsh policies of neo-liberalism' (2019 [2000]: 254–255).

We Are The Lions Mr Manager, my first case study, returns us to the late seventies and the inception of 'the great moving right show' to reflect on how socialist feminism's connection to a 'wider movement of resistance' might be instructive for our present 'populist moment'. What this performance dramatises is the two-year strike (August 1976–July 1978) at the Grunwick film-processing laboratories in Willesden (London Borough of Brent) by Asian women workers and their charismatic leader Jayaben Desai. Class, gender and race intersected in this struggle for the workers' right to be unionised and to be treated with dignity in the workplace. Its popular-political staging by the Townsend Theatre company in a touring production (2017–2018) is one that I approach as a countercultural intervention into the reclaiming of an historic struggle that mobilised a 'chain of equivalence' between immigrant, socialist and feminist constituencies. It is possible that commemorating a past struggle might be perceived as a nostalgic act of retrieval and readily dismissed as such. But as Rowbotham contends, when the sociopolitical circumstances are such that the 'promise of a dream' is broken, the vision of a radicalised democracy shattered, 'claiming space to remember' can serve as 'an act of rebellion': it 'not only defies an overtly guarded set of political assumptions but also touches the sources of desire' (2019 [2000]: xv). By 'claiming space to remember' Grunwick through an affective mode of popular-political engagement, *We Are The Lions Mr Manager* reanimates the political 'sources of desire' that mobilised the strike and thereby potentially ignites present yearnings for a great moving *left* show.

Where the socialist-feminist 'dream' of 'democratizing daily life' through the structural transformation of social, economic and patriarchal subordination formerly faced antagonisms from the left (and right), thereafter it had to contend not only with the nightmare of feminism's neoliberal double but also, as headlined in Chapter 1, what Beatrix Campbell outlines as the formation of an aggressively anti-democratic 'neopatriarchal and neoliberal matrix' (2013: 91). Introducing her manifesto *End of Equality*, Campbell paraphrases Marx's *Manifesto of the Communist Party* by substituting 'woman' as the 'sceptre [that] is haunting' the world, a 'spectre' that 'the powers of old Europe and the old world have entered into a holy alliance to exorcise' (ibid.: 1). In closing, she protests that 'it is high time that feminism meets this myth of the "Spectre of Feminism" with its own new manifestos' (ibid.: 92). What form new socialist-feminist manifestos might take at this critical conjuncture is exemplified by her own declaration rooted in Marxism, feminism and environmentalism, through which she arrives at a counter-hegemonic, non-sexist, non-violent, socially egalitarian and ecologically aware vision:

> Imagine men without violence. Imagine sex without violence. Imagine that men stop stealing our stuff – our time, our money and our bodies; imagine societies that share the costs of care, that share the costs of everything; that make cities fit for children; that renew rather than wreck and waste. (ibid.)

Historically, an eco-grammar was not part of the socialist-feminist lexicon. But increasingly, from a socialist-feminist perspective the connections between neopatriarchal-neoliberal capitalism's exploitation of women's productive, socially reproductive and care-giving labour, and its exploitative abuse of natural resources that it mines, drains but does not replenish, cannot be ignored. In my second case study, *Escaped Alone* (2016), it is Caryl Churchill's eco-socialist feminism that I set out to explore: her apocalyptic vision of a neoliberal world in ecological and social meltdown performed by an ensemble of four older women. Book-ending the canonical *Top Girls* (1982) in which Churchill critiqued the idea of feminism without socialism, *Escaped Alone* recounts the dystopian future that awaits if a socially progressive solution to the crisis of neoliberalism cannot be found.

We Are The Lions Mr Manager: The Great Moving Left Show

In their manifesto *Feminism for the 99%*, Cinzia Arruzza et al. identify a 'new wave of militant feminist activism' evidenced by the 'international feminist and women's strikes of 2017 and 2018' (2019: 5). Tracing the origin of the strikes back to the 2016 protest in Poland over the banning of abortion in that country, the authors detail how women's strikes in different nations gathered momentum and on International Women's Day in 2017 crystallised into a 'transnational movement' (ibid.: 6–7). They observe that such strikes are '[r]e-animating' the 'militant spirit' of earlier working-class women's struggles: 'the feminist strikes of today are reclaiming our roots in historic struggles for workers' rights and social justice' (ibid.: 7). Where these strikes are seen to be 're-animating' the 'militant spirit' of past protests, my claim in this case study of *We Are The Lions Mr Manager* is that *performing* 'historic struggles for workers' rights and social justice' can be instructive for contemporary anti-capitalist, socialist-feminist demonstrations (in all senses) of opposition to the economic inequalities and injustices of neoliberalism.

My initial interest in the cultural representation of strikes by women was piqued by *Made in Dagenham*, the film (2010) and stage musical (2014), which portrayed the historic strike by women in 1968 at Dagenham's Ford car factory, industrial action that lead to the 1970 Equal Pay Act (Aston 2016). The popular-feminist format of the women-friendly show portraying an activist protest by working-class women is one that I encountered again in Maxine Peake's *Queens of the Coal Age*, first broadcast as a radio play (BBC Radio 4, 2013) and then adapted for the stage (Royal Exchange Theatre, Manchester, 2018). What Peake's drama commemorated and celebrated was the occupation of Parkside Colliery in 1993 by four women from the mining community protesting against further pit closures in an industry that had been decimated since the miner's strike in 1984. Shows such as these that evidence a commitment to the cultural transmission of 'important historical moments of liberation' are valuable to creating 'new radical imaginaries' (McRobbie 2009: 49). As Angela McRobbie contends, a culturally transmitted 'memorialised history of past struggles' is one that might serve as a 'resource, a source of hope, a space that offers vocabularies, concepts, histories, narratives, and experiences' to aid us in 'overcoming' a present 'predicament or powerlessness' (ibid.).[3] Writing *The Aftermath of Feminism* published in 2009, McRobbie was concerned about 'the shutting down' of such resources and the disarticulation of radical, socially progressive histories that occurred when these were 'caricatured and trivialised' (ibid.). But at the close of this decade, when I think of the burgeoning of anti-capitalist, socialist-feminist theatre that I have written about elsewhere (Aston 2018), or of *Made in Dagenham* and other British films such as *Pride* (2014), *Suffragette* (2015), and *Peterloo* (2018), all of which portray the unforgetting of an historic struggle against injustices and inequalities, then I feel cautiously optimistic about the countercultural resourcing of 'radical imaginaries'.

The contribution that Townsend Theatre makes to the re-articulation of past struggles is through a repertoire devoted entirely to working-class histories—histories of class injury routinely hidden from the historical-cultural mainstream. Established in 2011 by director/producer Louise

Townsend and writer/performer Neil Gore, the company to-date has dramatised: *The Ragged Trousered Philanthropists* (2011–2013; 2015); *We Will Be Free!*, the story of the Tolpuddle Martyrs (2013–2014); *United We Stand!*, based on the Shrewsbury pickets (2014–2016); *Dare Devil Rides to Jarama*, on the International Brigade and the Spanish Civil War (2016–2017); *We Are The Lions Mr Manager* (2017–2018) and *Rouse, Ye Women!* a show about trade unionist Mary Macarthur and the women chainmakers' strike in 1910 (2019).

Directed by Townsend and written by Gore, like most of the company's shows *We Are The Lions Mr Manager* is scripted for two performers: Medhavi Patel played Desai and Gore role-played the multiple male figures involved in the strike—adversaries and supporters. Formally and stylistically, the show records Grunwick through conventions, techniques and dynamics indebted to the popular-political, alternative theatre tradition that burgeoned in the seventies. Its style is presentational rather than representational; the strike is retold through an episodic montage of scenes composed in two acts and interspersed with union songs performed live by Gore under the direction of folk musician, John Kirkpatrick. As politically committed theatre in the alternative tradition, during its seven-month national tour the show played in non-theatre spaces (such as libraries, workers' institutes, or community centres), regional theatres and fringe venues like Brighton Festival's Old Court Room. Significantly, given the subject matter of the show, it also had two stagings at London's multicultural Tara Theatre.[4]

Townsend's audiences therefore range from constituencies for whom the social histories the company presents are of specialist interest (especially given the links the group has forged with trades unions and councils) and more regular theatre-goers in regional venues. I caught the show on 10 February 2018 in the studio space at Harrogate Theatre.[5] This is not a venue on my theatre radar but, given the relatively out-of-the-way places the company tours to, the North Yorkshire town of Harrogate was the most accessible option from my Lancashire base. A wealthy spa town and Conservative stronghold since the 2010 General Election, Harrogate seems an unlikely home for Townsend's socialist and feminist repertoire, but the company are regulars there—an indication, perhaps, that their work does not play only to the politically converted.

Casting an eye over the audience at the Saturday matinee I attended, my impression was that a significant number of spectators were old enough to have encountered the Grunwick dispute through its high-profile media coverage in the seventies. It was during the summer of 1977 when the strike action escalated through mass picketing and a Day of Action (11th July) that Grunwick became 'a dominant media *cause célèbre*'; the dispute achieved 'iconic national status' as 'a focal point for contested explanations and proposed remedies for' the 'disease' of antagonistic relations between workers and management (McGowan 2008: 384). As Amrit Wilson, writer, activist and supporter of the strike, observes, the media reporting was biased in its portrayal of the dispute: 'For example, BBC Television on the evening of the 11th July, Day of Action, and the papers next morning were full of pictures of injured policemen, but the pickets who were injured were hardly mentioned' (2018 [1978]: 79). Reporting on the strike and its media coverage in the August issue of *Spare Rib*, Campbell and Val Charlton outlined the dispute for their feminist readership (Campbell and Charlton 1977). Specifically, they explained: the cause of the strike that lay in poor working conditions and unacceptably low wages (£28 for a 40 hour week); the workers' determination to exercise their right to be unionised (they joined APEX, The Association of Professional, Executive, Clerical and Computer Staff); the resistance to their unionisation by Grunwick boss, George Ward, backed by the right-wing NAFF (The National Association For Freedom); and the support for the strikers from Brent Trades Council (especially its Secretary, Jack Dromey), as well as the Labour Movement at large. In contrast to the media's focus on the policing of the strike or on prominent males in the Labour Movement, Campbell and Charlton foregrounded women's voices from within the Asian community of strikers, women's groups and the Women's Liberation Movement. Hence, their reporting showed the strike in a different light to the media: highlighted the struggle against capitalist exploitation and exposed the problem of patriarchalism that the Asian women experienced on all fronts—in their community, on the factory floor and the picket line.

We Are The Lions Mr Manager works in a comparable way to the feminist *Spare Rib* article. The show crams an abundant wealth of detail about the strike and its principle players into the multiple, quick-changing scenes (programme notes included a glossary of acronyms in case we got lost in the dizzy array of parties involved). With Desai/Patel as the herstorical witness to events, the dispute is staged from her standpoint rather than as refracted by the media. Indeed, there is one picket line scene in Act Two in which Desai/Patel is interviewed by and admonishes a BBC reporter/Gore for his prejudicial stance and patronising attitude to her striking community.

The matter of the strike's alignment with the Women's Liberation Movement is portrayed in Act One. Patel/Desai, standing next to a banner for the 'National Women's Liberation Conference', picks up a microphone to address us, the audience, as though at the conference, delivering a speech that touched on how badly the women had been treated in the workplace and the idea that her Asian community could play a full role in the Union movement.[6] Thus, it is Desai, the striking Asian female worker, who is portrayed as bridging the gap between feminism and the left: it was the strike that helped close the 'distance' 'between left wing politics and feminism' (Campbell and Charlton 1977: 46), as well as enabling socialist feminists to join the Asian women's community in activist protest and solidarity.[7]

The importance of this triangulation cannot be understated. This is not only because it invites us to remember how seminal this Asian women's strike is to histories of socialist and feminist trade union activism, but also for the reason that it challenges the image of seventies feminism as concerned exclusively with the interests of white, middle-class women. Equally and crucially, it exemplifies how a struggle communicated in a shared language of exploitation could overcome antagonisms between the left and feminism. As the show highlights, Desai expressed the Asian women's struggle as the fight for *all* workers to be treated with dignity in the workplace and to have the right to be unionised. In Mouffe's Gramscian terms, what this exemplifies is how the mobilisation of 'common affects in defence of equality and social justice' renders it possible to forge a 'chain of equivalence' among otherwise antagonistically situated constituencies (Mouffe 2018: 6). For instance, in the show's re-enactment of the build-up to the Day of Action in Act Two, projected documentary footage of the mass picketing offered a powerful reminder of how male-dominated, white-working-class sectors overcame sexist and racist attitudes by joining the fight for dignity and unionisation. Notably, this included the dockers, a sector who in 1968 had marched in support of Enoch Powell's anti-immigration, racist sentiments.[8]

At the time of Grunwick, the concept of intersectionality had not been formulated. Nonetheless, as Wilson explains, she and 'other Black feminists' recognised 'that experiences, and structural aspects of race, class and gender (and also for South Asians, caste) shaped each other' (2018 [1978]: xvii). Intersectional axes of oppression were demonstrable in the

Asian women workers' economic, social and racial disenfranchisement. As Wilson observed, these women were 'the worst off of all British workers': 'They are black so they need not be treated even like women, but more like animals' (ibid.: 59). In the performance, the two-hander casting of the white, male Gore and Asian, female Patel provides a constant reminder of the complexities of class, gender and race played out in the strike. White masculinity prevails throughout Gore's schizophrenic splits as he switches between the role of trade unionist, Dromey, an ardent supporter of the strike, and an adversary such as Malcolm Alden, manager of Grunwick's mail order department. The two-dimensional, emblematic playing of these roles captured the predominantly white masculine composition of the unionised left and the ranks of the reactionary right. Contrastingly, Patel remains fixed in her part, undertaking the role of Desai to render the essence of the charismatic leader of the strike who broke the racialised-gender stereotype of the passive, submissive Asian woman, a role that as a British-Asian actress and distant relative of Desai, she found personally and politically inspiring.[9]

However, there is one significant exception to this: in an episode that follows immediately after her speech to the women's conference, Patel doubles as Ward, the Anglo-Indian boss of Grunwick. Her cartoon rendering of the capitalist boss as she bulked out her body in an over-sized man's coat and appeared alongside an image of Thatcher and two union jacks,[10] gestured to the capitalist exploitation warring within and against the democratic 'body' which Desai represents. It also marked Ward's eschewal of any identification with the Asian workers on ethnic grounds—a possibility given his Anglo-Indian background. In fact, the opposite was the case: he exploited his familiarity with the customs and conventions of the community in attempts to control the women and prevent them from joining the strike (Wilson 2018 [1978]: 76–77); his verbal abuse of Desai and the women on the picket line is also depicted in the show, memorably as Patel/Desai mimicked Ward's mocking insistence that he see her on the picket line in a 'mini skirt, not a sari'.[11]

Since the character of Desai is our empathetic point of identification, her role as an eye witness to events is crucial for the show to succeed as a re-telling of a workers' struggle that aligned the socialist- and feminist-left, rather than as a biographical herstory. Thus, biographical details are kept to minimum; only the opening scene sketches background details, notably concerning Desai's educated, middle-class circumstances and relocation from Tanzania, East Africa to Britain in the late sixties, thereby marking the dissonance between her former life and life as an exploited worker in the UK. Above all, the show's recourse to Brechtian techniques mixed with the strike songs and a pantomime-style of audience engagement, helped to maintain the social eye as opposed to the autobiographical 'I'. To elaborate briefly: Patel repeatedly broke the fourth wall by addressing the audience directly and Gore's strike songs also served to interrupt the narrative flow. There was audience participation of the pantomimic kind as spectators were called up on stage to act as protesting strikers. And then there were Gore's frequent improvised interactions with spectators: those of us, me included, who booed too loudly at his cartoon policeman were jokingly told off for forgetting the pantomime season was over. The unity of the setting—the film-processing office with wire-mesh screens signifying the gates at which the picket-lines gathered—was disrupted through music, props and projections, used to index the multiple sites in which events took place. Documentary techniques were deployed to authenticate the 'truth' of what happened: projected footage of the Day of Action; placards bearing original strike slogans; political songs and verbatim speeches such as Desai's much-quoted reply to her Grunwick manager as she walked out of the workplace:

> What you are running here is not a factory, it is a zoo. But in a zoo there are many types of animals. Some are monkeys who dance on your fingertips, others are lions who can bite your head off. We are the lions, Mr Manager!'[12]

Also, because the two performers stage-managed every scene, their out-of-character labour revealed rather than concealed the making of the theatrical event. Like the labour of the strike itself, the performers' visible orchestration of events resonated with the sense of a strenuous and exhausting commitment to making something happen (with a running time of two hours, the 'sweat' of the performers' labour was visible by the close). Finally, there was the overall, cumulative effect of the episodic recounting of each of Desai's thwarted attempts to secure the workers' rights. If spectators know the history of Grunwick, then they know the outcome: ultimately, the strike failed due to the state, trade union leadership and Grunwick bosses colluding against its success.[13] But the episodic form and overall aesthetic of the show worked to elicit a critical sensing of the wrongs that could have been but were not righted. To borrow from Brecht, spectators were potentially left feeling: 'That's not the way – That's extraordinary, hardly believable – It's got to stop' (1964, 71).

Going to the show with my horizon of popular-political, Brechtian-influenced horizon of expectation, I had wondered whether the performance would succeed in its mission to historicise and politicise this historic struggle. Would this aesthetic that worked for the alternative, political theatre scene in the seventies work now or merely feel outdated? But I had underestimated how oppositional forms of theatre are renewed and revitalised in times of political crisis such as this populist conjuncture. As Derek Paget observes in his illuminating exposition of the appearances and disappearances of documentary theatre, alternative forms of political theatre belong to a 'broken tradition' (2009: 224). They are taken up as 'weapons' in 'political struggles' but 'recede' when 'crises pass' (ibid.: 224–225). He further notes that: 'Theatre in this vein needs also a different kind of creative energy, and energy is not a limitless commodity' (ibid.: 225). In short, as a 'commodity' political theatre is subject to supply and demand: a countercultural resource or 'weapon' against oppression supplied when there is a renewed demand for oppositional forms of performance whose 'creative energy' aspires to generate social energies in and beyond the theatre.

Theatre forged in the popular-political theatre tradition typically responds to oppression by establishing a Gramscian front or frontier between oppressed and oppressor, between 'us' and 'them'. *We Are The Lions Mr Manager* is no exception, not least because it 'entertains' a strike situation defined by the frontier between workers and bosses, the exploited and the exploiters. That frontier also shapes spectators' relationship to and engagement with the show: entering the agit-prop spirit of the performance means joining the workers in the fight against the bosses. If you were not shouting along with Desai/Patel's chanting of 'we want a union', then you were siding with management/Gore's demand to break the strike by returning to work. Towards the close of the show, Desai/Patel recounts just how fierce the strength of opposition to the women's demand for 'basic rights' was at the time of Grunwick: opposition from the bosses, the media, the police, the courts, the government ('faces like stone'). Hence, in a final monologue she insists on the importance of 'determined struggle' and 'total solidarity' in the fight against 'injustice'.

In today's austerity Britain, establishing a 'political frontier' between 'the people' and 'the oligarchy' is essential to create 'the type of politics needed to recover and deepen democracy' (Mouffe 2018: 5). As Mouffe elaborates, this requires a struggle on multiple fronts, many of which lie 'outside the productive process' (ibid.: 6), such as the renewed radical-feminist struggles against patriarchalism detailed in Chapter 3. That said, it is nonetheless the case that the 'productive process', the lynchpin of Marxist analysis, remains a significant site of struggle. The deepening exploitation of women and men in the neoliberal workplace has seen increasing numbers of workers in low-paid, often non-unionised, sectors treated without dignity. Factor race into the picture of neoliberal Britain's low-paid (or unemployed) workforce and the inequalities worsen, as Reni Eddo-Lodge's analysis of census data on race and poverty demonstrates (2018 [2017]: 193–194). Moreover, not only is it the case that BAME 'women are more likely to be unemployed than white women' (ibid.: 193), but research on racism at work conducted by the Trades Union Congress in 2017 showed '2 in 5 (41%)' of BAME women 'wanted to leave their jobs because of bullying and harassment, but could not afford to' (TUC 2017).

In brief, to recognise these racialised and gendered inequalities is to see the 'productive process' as a site that remains critical to the fight for democracy. By moving Desai and the story of Grunwick centre stage, *We Are The Lions Mr Manager* elicits past-present connections to this struggle, exemplifying the ongoing need for the linkages between the trade union movement, socialist and feminist movements. Moreover, the show's 'striking' image of Desai's 'determined struggle' and its recollection of the Asian women who resisted patriarchal domination in the home to join the fight for dignity in the workplace, is a salutary reminder that today's revitalised feminist movement must not be reduced to an anti-democratic enclave of white, top-girl privilege.

Escaped Alone and the 'Dialectical Shock of Recognition'

From the sixties 'promise of a dream', through the decades of neoliberalism to the 'populist moment' and the tears in the neoliberal 'cladding', Caryl Churchill has evidenced a steadfast commitment to recitals of socialism and feminism. In the eighties, she expressed her concern about the direction feminism might be taking: as a committed socialist feminist, she was troubled by the rise of feminism's neoliberal double (see Chapter 2);

she could not 'conceive of a right-wing feminism' (1987: 78). Furthermore, while she acknowledged that socialism and feminism were not 'synonymous', she felt 'strongly about both and wouldn't be interested in a form of one that didn't include the other' (ibid.). Hence, for Churchill, the counter-hegemonic project of 'democratizing daily life' must attend both to 'economic class relations' and their 'patriarchal character'. Moreover, there is a further dynamic to her socialist-feminist outlook: the ecological. Hence, the triangulation of socialist, feminist and ecological dimensions renders Churchill's theatre a creative manifesto that makes an impassioned plea to address and redress the economic, social and environmental damage that capitalism produces.

Where Churchill's eco-socialist feminism is unwavering, the form her theatre takes evidences a remarkable degree of innovative alterability. And when the form shifts so do the means by which a mode of affectively rendered politicising engagement is achieved. However, Churchill's formal shapeshifting is undertaken always with a view to spectators feeling-seeing the political landscapes she dramatises: to achieving what Beverley Best terms the 'dialectical shock of recognition'—'a shift in the way one sees and perceives [that] produces a shift in the way one experiences and lives in the world' (2011: 81). Best postulates the 'dialectical shock of recognition' in relation to Marx's *Capital*, observing that Marx deployed a 'narrative strategy' that aimed at 'the production of affect' (ibid.). By means of a nonlinear narrative that moved between the 'abstract' and the 'concrete', *Capital* could elicit 'an affective response in the reader' when she experienced 'the shock of recognizing oneself in relation to the other, in relation to the social totality' (ibid.). Comparably, a drama such as *Top Girls* deploys a nonlinear narrative and a Brechtian repertoire of techniques to elicit an 'affective response' among spectators concerning the idea of feminism without socialism—an idea enacted by or concretised in the antagonistic relations and dialectical debate between the play's upwardly mobile Marlene and her working-class sister, Joyce. No less invested in the 'dialectical shock of recognition', *Escaped Alone* adopts a radically different form: eschews a Brechtian terrain in favour of an elliptically rendered treatment of neoliberal capitalism as the means by which the 'production of affect' might be achieved. In this instance, as I detail in the analysis that follows, a 'dialectical shock of recognition' hinges on techniques of disorientation to create an affective mode of engagement through which we might feel-see our way to understanding ourselves within (and against) a socially and ecologically damaging neoliberal-capitalist 'totality'.

Escaped Alone premiered Downstairs at the Royal Court Theatre in January 2016, directed by Churchill's long-term collaborator James Macdonald and designed by Miriam Buether. It was revived at the Court in January 2017 for a second run before a New York transfer and short national tour; it was also broadcast on BBC Radio 4 (2 June 2018). Like *Top Girls*, *Escaped Alone* has an all-female cast; exceptionally, the play's four women characters '*are all at least seventy*' (Churchill 2016: 4), thus representing a welcome redress to the paucity of roles for older actresses. Three of the four women—Sally (Deborah Findlay), Vi (June Watson) and Lena (Kika Markham)—constitute a circle of friends. The fourth woman Mrs Jarrett/Mrs J (Linda Bassett) initially is on the outside of this circle. Standing in front of a large garden fence that stretched the width of the Court's proscenium arch and directly addressing the audience, Bassett/Mrs J explained: 'I'm walking down the street and there's a door in the fence open and inside are three women I've seen before' (ibid.: 5). She joins the women in Sally's backyard, but unlike the trio of women who remain seated in the suburban garden, she periodically steps outside to deliver a series of monologues. There are eight garden scenes each punctuated by a monologue, the latter voiced by Bassett from a darkened stage surrounded by dual, rectangular frames of glowing electric light.

The design of the brightly lit garden, complete with fence, wooden shed, lawn, foliage and an assortment of chairs, provides a stark contrast to the void from which Mrs J speaks. The former setting is estranged by its juxtaposition with the latter: a technique of scenic dislocation that disturbs the familiarity of the garden. Reading *Promise of a Dream*, I encountered Rowbotham's adoption of the term *dépayser* (to disorientate) when recollecting her youthful desire to achieve a 'profound disorientation' from her everyday circumstances and through reading left-wing literature to seek a 'heightened state of becoming, seeing what had never been seen' (2019 [2000]: 8).[14] This lingered in my memory as I turned to re-reading *Escaped Alone* since the idea of *dépaysement* (disorientation/*feeling* of strangeness) captures the sensation of strangeness that Churchill's theatre has the power to evoke: a sense of disorientation through which an alternate mode of 'seeing' what has not 'been seen' might be possible. More specifically, as headlined above, in *Escaped Alone* techniques of *dépaysement* are a means to generate altered states of political perception: an affective recognition of the social inequalities, economic injustices and ecological damage caused by neoliberal capitalism. In short, to borrow from Okri, the play invites us to 'look beneath the cladding' to see the life-threatening, apocalyptic void it conceals in the hope that we might desire a political change of scene.

In the scenes set in the garden, the women make small talk about their families, friends and neighbourhood. They chat about the past, anchoring memories in inconsequential but personally significant details: hats worn at a wedding; shops that closed or changed their line of business; or how much a weekly shop cost pre-decimalisation. At all times, Churchill's positively minimalist lines of dialogue disorientate the production of coherent and linear meaning. These elliptically formed conversations proceed by associative connections so that a spectator has to fill in the gaps between what is said and left unsaid and keep track of conversational particles that make up atoms of meaning.

Although the tenor of the women's exchanges is light and frequently funny, there is an undercurrent of negative, anxious feelings. The staging of the play's later scenes saw the conversational flow of the group cease; the lighting dimmed on the group who remained frozen for an individual woman to soliloquise her fears and anxieties. What these moments elucidate is that the women's power of acting (in the Spinozan sense) is seriously diminished by negative affects: Sally suffers from a fear of cats; Lena from agoraphobia; and Vi from the 'horror' of having killed her husband in the kitchen, a 'horror' that 'goes on' because of 'not seeing' the son whose father she killed (ibid.: 41). Each of these anxiety states figures a dimension of Churchill's eco-socialist-feminist critique: domestic violence (Vi); the capitalist workplace where Lena was a 'high flying' professional (ibid.: 32); and a world of predatory behaviour that Sally projects on to the feline species, a phobic projection that also raises questions about human and non-human relations.[15] In short, these anxious voicings can all be diagnosed as the product of a capitalist system: the 'horror' of its predacious, violent culture which 'kills' the women's joy of home and (former) workplace.

This diagnosis is strengthened by Mrs J's voicing from the void, where, like a messenger in the biblical story of Job, she has 'escaped alone' to recount the apocalyptic destruction of the world. Seven times in seven monologues she tells the audience how people and the planet were destroyed by the elemental forces of earth, water, wind and fire—by pollution, hunger and sickness. However, these were neither god-sent nor natural disasters but the result of capitalism's exploitation of nature. When '[f]our hundred thousand tons of rock' crashed down a 'hillside to smash through the roofs, each fragment onto the designated child's head', this was 'paid for by senior executives' (ibid.: 8). '[W]ater was deliberately wasted in a campaign to punish the thirsty' (ibid.: 12), and the wind that 'turned heads inside out' had been 'developed by property developers' (ibid.: 28). And in a plague of ten fires, three were due to the 'spontaneous combustion of the markets' (ibid.: 37). In short, every ecological disaster can be traced back to capitalism that pollutes lives and wrecks planetary destruction.

Bassett did not emote these reports of cataclysmic events; there was no cathartic release of the classically conceived emotions of fear and pity to harmoniously return us to a social order. But nor was there a dialectical treatment of events: no contradictory forces to oppose what happened, as exemplified in *Top Girls* where the material conditions of a working-class woman like Joyce contradict her sister's neoliberal, 'top-girl' ethos. Instead, the cumulative effect of Bassett's liturgical emotionally detached narration of disaster heaped upon disaster potentially produced affective recognition of our stupefying attachment to neoliberal capitalism.

Disasters are told/foretold by Mrs J through Churchill's absurd, surreal images: of fires that 'consumed squirrels, firefighters and shoppers' (ibid.: 37); of '[b]uildings migrated from London to Lahore, Kyoto to Kansas City' (ibid.: 28); and of '[v]illages vanished and cities located to their rooftops' (ibid.: 12). Image upon surreal, poetically rendered image, builds another layer of *dépaysement*: a 'profound disorientation' from the idea that we can go on living as we are when the consequences are world-wide ecological and social destruction. Over the course of each monologue, what feels absurdly funny in one moment mutates into a darker note of social reckoning, and vice versa. As Matt Trueman observed in his review for *Variety*: 'She [Bassett] veers from humor to horror, sentence by sentence, so that laughter catches you off-guard, or else continues on into awful events, plainly stated' (2016). Thus, I took no pleasure in hearing that domestic violence increased after 'chemicals' were 'released through cracks and the money' (Churchill 2016: 17), but moments later laughed at the idea of 'dog owners' having to clean up 'their pets' vomit', or risk being fined (ibid.).[16]

Reviewing the premiere of *Escaped Alone*, Michael Billington noted that this is by no means Churchill's first play 'to jolt us into an awareness of apocalypse', citing *The Skriker* (1994) and *Far Away* (2000) as earlier, seminal examples (2016). On this occasion, he found the affective 'jolt' into the recognition of a world hurtling towards extinction 'less effective' as the monologues went on (ibid.). In an opposite way to Billington, I experienced the monologic repeats as simultaneously energising and draining given the cumulative effect of being struck by the horrific-to-comic/comic-to-horrific images and yet fatigued by Mrs J's seemingly inexhaustible supply of surreal terrors. In *Ugly Feelings*, Sianne Ngai proposes 'stuplimity' as a term to describe the aesthetic experience of works that are 'astonishing' and 'fatiguing': where an 'affective relationship to enormous, stupefying objects [...] may seem similar to, but ultimately does not fall within the scope of, either the Kantian or the popular sublime' (2007: 270–271). While 'stuplimity' conjures up the sublime, it does so 'negatively, since we infuse it with thickness or even stupidity' (ibid.: 271). Comparably, in *Escaped Alone* Churchill renders capitalism as a 'stupefying object', the 'stupidity' of which thickens as line by line, monologue by monologue, the disasters pile up. Where the sublime is popularly conceived as an encounter with the magnificence of nature, Churchill's 'stuplime' is a confrontation with the ugliness of man-made ecological and social destruction.

The antithetical states of heightened emotion (astonishment) and a dulling of the senses (fatigue) also have a temporal mirroring. In the time-compressed monologues, the apocalyptic events appear to speed up, occurring with great velocity. Contrastingly, in the garden, where nothing out of the ordinary happens, time passes slowly over the course of several afternoons that feel like one '*continuous*' afternoon (Churchill 2016: 4). As an anxious Lena complains: 'It was half past three and all this time later it's twenty-five to four' (ibid.: 32). Furthermore, irrespective of whether time slows down and emotions dull, or time and emotion quicken, what transpires are states of 'suspended agency' generated by the negative affects of a 'stuplime' aesthetic (Ngai 2007: 12). In the garden, 'suspended agency' occurs when the women soliloquise and language 'thickens' through repetition that binds each woman to an anxiety state she may temporarily assuage but cannot fully overcome. For instance, the language in Sally's monologue (the longest of all the soliloquies) congeals into an obsessive-compulsive, recursive iteration of the 'horror' of cats.

Delivered by Findlay, this speech was 'stuplimely' surprising and fatiguing as she listed all the household places where the feline species might be hiding: 'under the bed in the wardrobe up on the top shelf', or 'in with the jam and honey' (Churchill 2016: 26). Over in the void, a sense of 'suspended agency' stems from the sense that the pattern of world-shattering capitalist destruction never breaks but repeats. As Mrs J catalogues the catastrophic events, it becomes clear that even when faced with wholesale extinction people are not moved to act in the interest of others but continue to trade in their self-preservation, viscerally captured in the surreal imaging of '[t]he obese' who 'sold slices of themselves until hunger drove them to eat their own rashers' (ibid.: 22). Thus, overall the void mirrors our own 'suspended agency': our diminished capacity to see the world as it really is and to determine on an alternate, democratically and ecologically motivated course of action.

With that in mind, in a more hopeful way Churchill's dramatisation of the quartet of septuagenarian women proposes women's neighbourly networking as a way of offering mutual care and support as opposed to a creed of self-centred individualism. The friendship forged between Sally, Vi and Lena has been sustained over the years. They bicker as friends often do; the plain-speaking Vi can push either Sally or Lena too hard to face up to their respective anxiety states, while Sally is less than kind when she undermines Lena's unfilled desire to go to Japan with her retort of 'get to Tesco first' (ibid.: 41). But their friendship runs deeper than these commonplace frictions: notably, it was Sally who came to Vi's defence in court with an 'economical' version of the truth to support her friend's plea of self-defence, a version that 'took into account' what the violent husband was like (ibid.: 34). And while the less vocal Lena struggles to engage in the conversation, being part of the group is clearly vital to her day-to-day survival.

The support the women offer each other is love of sorts, but not the romantic kind. Referencing Archibald MacLeish's 1958 play *J.B.* which represented Job as a prosperous banker, Churchill credited MacLeish for presenting 'the possibility of rebuilding from the rubble of a bombed world on the foundation of love' (1960: 443). But she rejected his idea of 'individual love' (MacLeish's Job ultimately finds consolation in his wife) as compensation for the 'failure' to build an alternative to a world of capitalist misery (ibid.). Hence, in *Escaped Alone* the 'foundation' of a different social order resides in the idea of the women's reciprocal care-giving.

To be intimately bonded through the giving and receiving of care is core to social relations, yet as Kathleen Lynch et al. observe, 'the affective system' of providing 'love, care and solidarity' can be seriously diminished by the inequalities produced by the 'economic', 'political' and 'socio-cultural' systems with which it intersects (2009: 3). By way of exemplification: to think back again to *Top Girls* is to remember how Marlene's determination to succeed in the corporate workplace means that she foregoes the care of her daughter, Angie; the burden of childcare and the opportunity not just to care for but to care about Angie falls to her sister, Joyce. Thus, 'love, care and solidarity' break down between Marlene and Joyce not just because of their social, economic and political differences but also as a consequence of the maldistribution of affective (care-giving) labour. And as Angie prophetically declares in the final, one-word line of the play, this renders the future 'frightening' (Churchill 1982: 43).

Contrastingly, in *Escaped Alone*, despite their social differences—Sally and Lena come from the professional classes, Vi was a hairdresser and Mrs J a former lollipop lady—an egalitarian distribution of affective labour keeps the women together. In one way, this resonates with the 'love, care and solidarity' that socialist feminism has aspired to build across different social constituencies and classes of women. In another, the women's regular, care-giving 'occupation' of the garden (a kind of peaceful sit-in) serves to counteract neoliberal capitalism's 'stuplime' indifference to human and planetary welfare. Moreover, despite the negative affects produced by their anxiety states, the women's supportive care of each other means that they have not lost the capacity to experience joy. In Scene Six, unexpectedly and surprisingly, the women break into an acapella rendition of the pop song 'da doo ron ron' and 'stuplimity' gives way to the sublime (in the ordinary rather than philosophical sense). It was the one episode of joyous release in *Escaped Alone*: voices soared and spirits lifted in this collectively realised burst of happiness as the women sang for and with each other.

In contrast to this outburst of joy, towards the close of the play suppressed anger ignites as Mrs J soliloquises in the garden, repeating two words over and over again: 'terrible rage' (2016: 42). No explanation is offered. The causal connection between the seven monologues delivered in the void and the anger that resounds through the rhythmic repeating of the words in this final soliloquy is ours to make. This is arguably a rage-fuelled response to all the global destruction Mrs J has witnessed and recounted—horrific events that spark no ordinary 'rage' but a '*terrible* rage' the magnitude of which is evoked through the 25 times the words are repeated. Repetitiously stated, Mrs J's rage might suggest another state of 'suspended agency' or paralysis. And yet, as Ngai observes via a citation of Lacan in her theorisation of 'stuplimity', 'repetition demands the new' (2007: 262). Thus, to be affected by and identify with Mrs J's 'terrible rage' is to feel a paralysing sense of anger as disasters repeat and repeat, but also the potential elicitation of a rageful, political demand for a 'new', socially egalitarian and ecologically responsible system.

To identify with Mrs J's rage presupposes we find her a credible witness to the events she has told/foretold. Increased scepticism about the verbal 'cladding' politicians and financiers deploy to conceal escalating social inequalities and injustices lends sincerity to the apocalyptic voicings of this ordinary, working-class, ageing woman. Dressed in her loosely hanging mac and baggy leggings, Bassett/Mrs J presents as an everywoman genealogically connected to the comic tradition of the insignificant individual who comes up against a larger system: a representative of the 'flabby masses' antithetical to 'an oppressive system's fantasies of phallic virility' (Ngai 2007: 295). Thus, the veracity of Churchill's everywoman is never in doubt: she speaks truth to the power of an 'oppressive system', voices a deep-seated, political anger against its stupefying indifference to planetary destruction.

The world does not transform in *Escaped Alone* but goes on as before: Mrs J tells us she goes home after thanking the women for tea and the afternoons in the garden look set to repeat. However, the 'shadow comes up earlier' and the 'sun's gone' (Churchill 2016: 42), a closing reminder that time is running out to halt global ecological meltdown by transforming the neoliberal-capitalist system that produces it.[17]

Final Reflections on Restaging Feminisms

The rageful anger expressed by Churchill's Mrs J is the emotion that prevails throughout *Restaging Feminisms.* More specifically, what crashes through the performances case-studied in the chapters is a wave of feminist-political anger. When assembled and viewed together, the shows evince the muscle memory of capitalist and patriarchal injuries that stretch back in time—over decades and centuries. The expression of feminist anger testifies to the way in which the last forty years of neoliberalism have seen the promised 'dream' of mid-twentieth-century social democracy broken: how instead of progressing women's rights neoliberalism has delivered the 'end of equality'. Equally, the performances highlight how the centuries-long backstory of patriarchalism has continued to the detriment of many women's lives: there has been no end to the inequalities and abuses of the patriarchal set-up. Thus, collectively, the shows constitute a creative manifesto that variously advocates: an end to neoliberal choice feminism (*Home, I'm Darling*); justice for rape victims in the legal system (*Consent*); freedom from male violence against women (*The Suppliant Women*); the demand for equality and diversity in cultural and artistic representation (*Emilia*); the demand for workers' dignity (*We Are The Lions Mr Manager*); and an end to neoliberal capitalism's planetary destruction (*Escaped Alone*). By no means an exhaustive list of issues or demands, this inventory highlights the artistic representation of several feminist concerns that are seminal to 'the type of politics needed to recover and deepen democracy' (Mouffe 2018: 5).

What the shows also embody is the muscle memory of the feminisms forged by the seventies women's movement: the reanimation of liberal-, radical- and socialist-feminist dynamics. Each chapter-based re-encounter with liberal, radical and socialist feminism involved the critical strategy of folding the past into present feminist claims to more socially progressive futures. In the case of liberal feminism, what emerged as critical was the need to disarticulate the reinvention of equality-focused liberal feminism as choice feminism: to subject the freedom of the self-empowered, individual woman vaunted by neoliberalism to feminist scrutiny, exemplified by Laura Wade's critique of the 'darling' doll's house as a fantasy of white, middle-class privilege. Further, while acknowledging that there is an ongoing need to campaign and legislate for women's rights, the necessity to recognise the *limits* of what can be accomplished by equality-focused goals also was advocated. As Nina Raine highlights in *Consent*, equality before the law cannot be achieved unless the patriarchalism structured through the judicial system is transformed. The principle of transforming structures of social and economic subordination obtains for all institutions, organisations or industries, including the British theatre industry where campaigns for equality, an end to sexual harassment, class and intersectional oppressions are vigorously being fought (Chapter 1). In brief, it is at the limits of what equality-focused liberal feminism can achieve that the transformative ends of and need for radical and/or socialist feminisms come into view.

Given that the three-year timeline of *Restaging Feminisms* (2016–2019) crosses the Weinstein watershed, it is not surprising to encounter a resurgence of radical-feminist sentiments. Chapter 3 headlined how the anti-patriarchal stance formerly forged by radical feminism was rekindled through the #Me Too movement: the chorus of voices protesting 'Me Too' attests to the upsurge of women's widely felt, shared experience and recognition of male privilege and the abuse of power. Thus, as David Greig's rendition of *The Suppliant Women* intersected with the Weinstein watershed, so the production history and reception of the play became a complex site of feminist scrutiny and enquiry. Greig's revival of a classical Greek drama themed on male violence against women in which the female chorus is situated both *within* and *against* the patriarchal set-up, was presented in Chapter 3 beside the companion study of Morgan Lloyd Malcolm's all-female production of *Emilia*, the latter highlighting the feminist demand to move women's stories centre stage. With its comic deflation of the canonicity accorded to Shakespeare, Malcolm's play exemplifies a critical-creative resistance to British theatre's cultural malestream. Moreover, her intersectional approach to the writing and staging of *Emilia* is one that ensures an 'every woman's story' is not re-scripted as one of white, able-bodied, class and gender privilege.

As outlined in this final chapter, it was at the intersection of class and gender that socialist feminism forged its production of Marxist-informed, feminist thinking. But what evolved in the seventies as a socialist-feminist commitment to 'democratizing daily life' has been systematically eroded throughout the decades of a 'neopatriarchal and neoliberal' system. Recitals of socialist feminism therefore reprise a counter-hegemonic commitment to a socially egalitarian vision of work and homelife as exemplified by Campbell's manifesto quoted in the introduction to this chapter. Further, by remembering and commemorating the historic strike by Asian women workers at Grunwick, *We Are The Lions Mr Manager* serves to connect those past struggles for dignity and economic justice in the workplace to present abject conditions experienced by poorly-paid workers, BAME women significant among them. While the issue of addressing how the material conditions of many women's lives are adversely affected by the inequalities perpetuated by a neopatriarchal neoliberalism remains pivotal to socialist feminism, Churchill's *Escaped Alone* also impresses the need for an eco-dimension to an anti-capitalist stance in order to protest and end capitalist exploitation of life-sustaining, natural resources.

This recapitulation of the performances studied in *Restaging Feminisms* reminds us that as the feminist dynamics re-circulate on the British stage (as well as offstage in the campaigns agitating for change to the industry), they appear in a heterogenous mix of genres and styles: the comedy or ideas play in the realist tradition; the community-orientated classic; the memory play; the popular-political show; and the experimentally formed drama. Equally diverse are the venues the shows are performed in, ranging from small-scale touring venues through the high-profile subsidised sector to the commercial West End. Thus, my horizon of feminist-theatre expectation is no longer largely confined to the small-scale touring circuit as it was in the eighties; only *We Are The Lions Mr Manager* follows in the footsteps of the alternative socialist and feminist tradition.

This heterogeneity means that no one form, or type of venue, is privileged above all others. In this regard, I have endorsed Mouffe's advocacy of the multiple 'possible forms of *critical* art' (2013: 91; original emphasis). Although Mouffe does not exemplify her analysis by addressing the medium of theatre as such, her notion of counter-hegemonic, heterogeneously formed and differently sited 'critical' artistic works is one that I have extended to this theatre-focused study and its elucidation of the feminisms and their restaging. Tracing the different feminist dynamics and their theatrical formations provided a means to analyse 'the different ways in which artistic practices can contribute to unsettling the dominant hegemony' (ibid.). In each chapter, analysis of the criticality of feminist dynamics and the 'artistic practices' through which they are rendered was undertaken to posit each performance as making a counter-hegemonic contribution to 'unsettling the dominant hegemony', whether this was Wade's disarticulation of neoliberal choice feminism, or Churchill's critique of neoliberal capitalism's planetary destruction. Overall, as the case studies unfold, one after the other, I hope this achieves the desired, cumulative effect of seeing each performance as a link in a connecting chain that protests the 'end of equality' and articulates the possibility of more socially democratic, feminist futures.

Irrespective of genre, style or venue, the potential political efficacy of all the theatre explored in *Restaging Feminisms* resides in its capacity to generate the 'production of [feminist] ideas with the power to affect' (Mouffe 2018: 75). Thus, we might recall the affectively rendered 'shock of recognition' that accompanies Clare Perkins' tirade against patriarchal injury in the final monologue of *Emilia*; the viscerally voiced demand by the community chorus in *The Suppliant Women* that all women be granted equal power; or the proclamation of dignity in the workplace for all disenfranchised workers as rendered in the popular-political staging of

We Are The Lions Mr Manager. In short, the politicising pulse of the shows depends on creating *moving* impressions of feminism committed to equality and social justice.

The need for 'ideas with the power to affect' our capacity to act in the interests of democracy and for *all* socially progressive fronts to form links in the chain of equivalent struggles, is urgent and critical if we are ever to achieve the great moving left show. Otherwise, what awaits is the dystopian future that everywoman Mrs J bears witness to. The one-word, final line of Churchill's *Top Girls* feels chillingly apposite: 'Frightening'.

Acknowledgments I am grateful to literary agent Faith Evans for steering me in the direction of Sheila Rowbotham's *Promise of a Dream*.

Notes

1. The socialist-feminist vision of shared domestic labour is one that the coda to Laura Wade's *Home, I'm Darling* invokes; see Chapter 1.
2. For an overview, see Lovenduski and Randall's chapter on 'Difference, Identity, and Equality' that situates the evolution of socialist-feminist theorising alongside that of radical feminism and the rise of identity politics (1993: 57–92).
3. McRobbie's point is exemplified by the two community artworks that were commissioned to commemorate the 40th anniversary of Grunwick. These were completed and unveiled in 2017. Both murals are sited in Dollis Hill: one in Chapter Road close to the tube station; the other on the bridge on Dudden Hill Lane. Setting out to see the murals on a cold Sunday morning in November 2019, I experienced them as colourful collages that capture the spirit of the workers' struggle and the forces arraigned against them—as vibrant reminders of an historic strike that governmental neoliberalism would sooner see forgotten.
4. After a sold-out run at Tara Theatre in November 2017, the show returned in May 2018 as part of 'I'll Say It Again!', a festival of work hosted to celebrate the centenary of women's suffrage.
5. This was on the eve of wide-scale industrial action by British universities over the threat to pensions, a strike that turned into 'the worst industrial action at universities in modern times' (Woolcock 2018). Thus, my viewing of the show was affectively charged by the strike situation in which, as a member of the University and College Union, I was caught up in.
6. Campbell and Charlton report that Desai spoke at the Working Women's Charter Conference in 1977. They also explain how on the eve of the Day of Action women at a socialist-feminist conference held in London

agreed to co-ordinate efforts to make feminist support of the strike more visible among the rank and file of the predominantly male left.

7. Regarding the matter of a dialogue between feminists and the strikers, Wilson insightfully reflects that the *Spare Rib* article by 'white feminist reporters' was 'good' because the strike represented a 'common interest, a sort of shared experience which is understood by both sides, so people can talk freely' (2018 [1978]: 183). Contrastingly, 'if the same Asian women were being interviewed by the same feminists about their family life and feelings', then it would not have been 'possible for Asian women to be so frank or so open' (ibid.).
8. On the issue of the dockers' support of Powell, Rowbotham recollects: 'On 23 April [1968] I was going home to Hackney, sitting on the top of the bus, musing, when I caught sight of a clump of working-class men huddling defensively near the Houses of Parliament – East End dockers supporting Powell. I looked at them with a heavy heart. I would normally have seen a workers' demonstration and felt support. But this time we were on opposing sides and it hurt' (2019 [2000]: 172–173).
9. The role earned Patel a nomination as Best Theatre Actress in the Eastern Eye Arts, Culture & Theatre Awards (2018). In a press release, she stated: 'As an actress from a BAME background, traditionally the roles that are available to us can be limiting. Too often Indian women can be typecast as the subservient housewives, mothers and suppressed daughters, so to play an iconic and strong leader from a Gujarati background has been a true blessing' (qtd. in Cox 2018).
10. The image of Thatcher gestured to the imminent 'great moving right show' that followed in the wake of James Callaghan's Labour government under which the strike took place.
11. All citations from *We Are The Lions Mr Manager* are taken from the live performance; there is no published script.
12. This speech was published in the programme notes.
13. For a detailed account, see McGowan (2008).
14. Rowbotham recollects coming across the term when reading Judith Okely's biography of Simone de Beauvoir: she cites Okely's description of a young de Beauvoir reading 'as a means of translating herself into other worlds, employing "the word *dépayser* (to change scenery or disorientate) to describe what they did for her"' (2019 [2000]: 8).
15. For a full discussion of Churchill's 'dark ecology' and the damaged relations between human and non-human worlds, see Aston (2015).
16. British dog owners are a 'breed' required by law to clean up after their pets in public grounds.
17. Since 2018, protests over climate change have gathered significant momentum, notably through the global movements School Strike for the Climate and Extinction Rebellion.

Works Cited

Arruza, C., T. Bhattacharya, and N. Fraser. 2019. *Feminism for the 99%: A Manifesto*. London: Verso.

Aston, E. 2015. Caryl Churchill's 'Dark Ecology'. In *Rethinking the Theatre of the Absurd: Ecology, the Environment and the Greening of the Modern Stage*, ed. C. Lavery and C. Finburgh, 59–76. London: Bloomsbury Methuen Drama.

———. 2016. Agitating for Change: Theatre and a Feminist 'Network of Resistance'. *Theatre Research International* 41 (1): 5–20.

———. 2018. Enter Stage Left: 'Recognition', 'Redistribution', and the A-Affect. *Contemporary Theatre Review* 28 (3): 299–309.

Best, B. 2011. 'Fredric Jameson Notwithstanding': The Dialectic of Affect. *Rethinking Marxism* 23 (1): 60–82.

Billington, M. 2016. Review of *Escaped Alone*. *Guardian*, 28 January. https://www.theguardian.com/stage/2016/jan/28/alone-together-review-caryl-churchill-royal-court-london.

Boughton, J. 2019. *Municipal Dreams: The Rise and Fall of Council Housing*. London: Verso.

Brecht, B. 1964. *Brecht on Theatre*, trans. J. Willett. London: Methuen.

Campbell, B. 2013. *End of Equality: The Only Way Is Women's Liberation*. London: Seagull.

Campbell, B., and V. Charlton. 1977. A Nice Power. *Spare Rib*, August, 6–7 and 46.

Churchill, C. 1960. Not Ordinary, Not Safe: A Direction for Drama? *The Twentieth Century*, November, 443–451.

———. 1982. *Top Girls*. London: Methuen.

———. 1987. Interview. In *Interviews with Contemporary Women Playwrights*, ed. K. Betsko and R. Koenig, 75–84. New York: Beech Tree Books.

———. 2016. *Escaped Alone*. London: Nick Hern.

Coote, A., and B. Campbell. 1982. *Sweet Freedom: The Struggle for Women's Liberation*. London: Picador.

Cox, A. 2018. Militant Medhavi Patel Gets Best Theatre Actress Nod at Eastern Eye Arts, Culture & Theatre Awards. *Stage Review*, 11 May. http://www.stagereview.co.uk/theatre-news/militant-medhavi-patel-gets-best-theatre-actress-nod-at-eastern-eye-arts-culture-theatre-awards/.

Eddo-Lodge, R. 2018 [2017]. *Why I'm No Longer Talking to White People About Race*. London: Bloomsbury.

Hall, S. 1988. *The Hard Road to Renewal: Thatcherism and the Crisis of the Left*. London: Verso.

Lovenduski, J., and V. Randall. 1993. *Contemporary Feminist Politics: Women and Power in Britain*. Oxford: Oxford University Press.

Lynch, K., J. Baker, and M. Lyons. 2009. *Affective Equality: Love, Care and Injustice*. Basingstoke: Palgrave Macmillan.

McGowan, J. 2008. 'Dispute', 'Battle', 'Siege', 'Farce'?—Grunwick 30 Years On. *Contemporary British History* 22 (3): 383–406.

McRobbie, A. 2009. *The Aftermath of Feminism: Gender, Culture and Social Change*. London: Sage.

Mouffe, C. 2013. *Agonistics: Thinking the World Politically*. London: Verso.

———. 2018. *For a Left Populism*. London: Verso.

Ngai, S. 2007. *Ugly Feelings*. Cambridge, MA: Harvard University Press.

Okri, B. 2017. Grenfell Tower, June, 2017: A Poem. *Financial Times*, 23 June. https://www.ft.com/content/39022f72-5742-11e7-80b6-9bfa4c1f83d2.

Paget, D. 2009. The 'Broken Tradition' of Documentary Theatre and Its Continued Powers of Endurance. In *Get Real: Documentary Theatre Past and Present*, ed. A. Forsyth and C. Megson, 224–238. Basingstoke: Palgrave Macmillan.

Rowbotham, S. 2019 [2000]. *Promise of a Dream: Remembering the Sixties*. London: Verso.

Trueman, M. 2016. Review of *Escaped Alone*. *Variety*, 29 January. https://variety.com/2016/legit/reviews/escaped-alone-review-caryl-churchill-1201692064/.

TUC. 2017. 1 in 3 British BME Workers Have Been Bullied, Abused or Singled Out for Unfair Treatment, Finds TUC Poll. *TUC* Website, 13 September. https://www.tuc.org.uk/news/1-3-british-bme-workers-have-been-bullied-abused-or-singled-out-unfair-treatment-finds-tuc-poll.

Wilson, A. 2018 [1978]. *Finding a Voice: Asian Women in Britain*, 2nd ed., n.p. Daraja Press.

Woolcock, N. 2018. University Lecturers to Strike as Students Sit Summer Exams. *The Times*, 9 March. https://www.thetimes.co.uk/article/university-lecturers-to-strike-as-students-sit-summer-exams-2jmmxlsbx.

Bibliography

Ahmed, S. 2005. The Non-Performativity of Anti-racism. *Borderlands* 5 (3) (e-journal).

———. 2010. *The Promise of Happiness*. Durham: Duke University Press.

Armstrong, S. 2017. *The New Poverty*. London: Verso.

Arruza, C., T. Bhattacharya, and N. Fraser. 2019. *Feminism for the 99%: A Manifesto*. London: Verso.

Arts Council England. 2017. Guide to Producing Equality Action Plans and Objectives for NPOs. https://www.artscouncil.org.uk/sites/default/files/download-file/Equality%20Action%20Guide%20-%20Introduction.pdf.

Aston, E. 1999. *Feminist Theatre Practice: A Handbook*. London: Routledge.

———. 2003. *Feminist Views on the English Stage: Women Playwrights, 1990–2000*. Cambridge: Cambridge University Press.

———. 2015. Caryl Churchill's 'Dark Ecology'. In *Rethinking the Theatre of the Absurd: Ecology, the Environment and the Greening of the Modern Stage*, ed. C. Lavery and C. Finburgh, 59–76. London: Bloomsbury Methuen Drama.

———. 2016. Agitating for Change: Theatre and a Feminist 'Network of Resistance'. *Theatre Research International* 41 (1): 5–20.

———. 2018. Enter Stage Left: 'Recognition', 'Redistribution', and the A-Affect. *Contemporary Theatre Review* 28 (3): 299–309.

Aston, E., and G. Harris. 2013. *A Good Night Out for the Girls*. Basingstoke: Palgrave Macmillan.

Auld, T. 2012. Angry Young Women: The New Generation of Young Female Playwrights. *Daily Telegraph*, 8 May. https://www.telegraph.co.uk/culture/theatre/theatre-features/9239192/Angry-young-women-the-new-generation-of-young-female-playwrights.html.

Bates, L. 2014. *Everyday Sexism*. London: Simon & Schuster.

E. Aston, *Restaging Feminisms*,
https://doi.org/10.1007/978-3-030-40589-2

Beard, M. 2017. *Women and Power: A Manifesto*. London: Profile Books.

Best, B. 2011. 'Fredric Jameson Notwithstanding': The Dialectic of Affect. Rethinking Marxism 23 (1): 60–82.

Billington, M. 2014. Speaking Truth to Power: This Is the Rebirth of Political Theatre. *Guardian*, 7 November. https://www.theguardian.com/commentisfree/2014/nov/07/rebirth-political-theatre-society-stage.

———. 2016. Review of *Escaped Alone*. *Guardian*, 28 January. https://www.theguardian.com/stage/2016/jan/28/alone-together-review-caryl-churchill-royal-court-london.

———. 2017. Love and Justice on Trial in Fierce Courtroom Drama. *Guardian*, 5 April. https://www.theguardian.com/stage/2017/apr/05/consent-review-nina-raine-dorfman-london-anna-maxwell-martin.

Bird, S. 2019. National Theatre Should Change Its Name After 'Ignoring' Women, Sandi Toksvig Says. *Telegraph*, 30 March. https://www.telegraph.co.uk/news/2019/03/30/national-theatre-should-change-name-ignoring-women-sandi-toksvig/.

Boughton, J. 2019. *Municipal Dreams: The Rise and Fall of Council Housing*. London: Verso.

Brecht, B. 1964. *Brecht on Theatre*, trans. J. Willett. London: Methuen.

Brown, M. 2016. Emma Rice to Step Down as Artistic Director at Shakespeare's Globe. *Guardian*, 25 October. https://www.theguardian.com/stage/2016/oct/25/emma-rice-step-down-artistic-director-shakespeares-globe.

———. 2018. Arts Industry Report Asks: Where Are All the Working-Class People? *Guardian*, 16 April. https://www.theguardian.com/culture/2018/apr/16/arts-industry-report-asks-where-are-all-the-working-class-people.

Butler, J. 2015. *Notes Toward a Performative Theory of Assembly*. Cambridge, MA: Harvard University Press.

Cameron, D. 2010. Big Society Speech. Gov.UK, 19 July. https://www.gov.uk/government/speeches/big-society-speech.

Campbell, B. 2013. *End of Equality: The only Way Is Women's Liberation*. London: Seagull.

Campbell, B., and V. Charlton. 1977. A Nice Power. *Spare Rib*, August, 6–7 and 46.

Case, S. 2008 [1988]. *Feminism and Theatre*. Basingstoke: Palgrave Macmillan.

Churchill, C. 1960. Not Ordinary, Not Safe: A Direction for Drama? *The Twentieth Century*, November, 443–451.

———. 1982. *Top Girls*. London: Methuen.

———. 1987. Interview. In *Interviews with Contemporary Women Playwrights*, ed. K. Betsko and R. Koenig, 75–84. New York: Beech Tree Books.

———. 2016. *Escaped Alone*. London: Nick Hern.

Clapp, S. 2017. Review of *The Suppliant Women*. *Guardian*, 26 November. https://www.theguardian.com/stage/2017/nov/26/the-suppliant-women-review-young-vic-aeschylus-david-greig.

Cochrane, K. 2013. The Fourth Wave of Feminism: Meet the Rebel Women. *Guardian*, 10 December. https://www.theguardian.com/world/2013/dec/10/fourth-wave-feminism-rebel-women.

Coote, A., and B. Campbell. 1982. *Sweet Freedom: The Struggle for Women's Liberation*. London: Picador.

Costa, M. 2017. Review of *The Suppliant Women*. *Exeunt Magazine*, 20 November. http://exeuntmagazine.com/reviews/the-suppliant-women-at-the-young-vic/.

Cox, A. 2018. Militant Medhavi Patel Gets Best Theatre Actress Nod at Eastern Eye Arts, Culture & Theatre Awards. *Stage Review*, 11 May. http://www.stagereview.co.uk/theatre-news/militant-medhavi-patel-gets-best-theatre-actress-nod-at-eastern-eye-arts-culture-theatre-awards/.

Crenshaw, K. 1989. Demarginalizing the Intersection of Race and Sex: A Black Feminist Critique of Antidiscrimination Doctrine, Feminist Theory and Antiracist Politics. *University of Chicago Legal Forum* 1 (8): 139–167.

Crompton, S. 2015. Interview, Rufus Norris: How the National Needs to Change. *Guardian*, 25 September. https://www.theguardian.com/stage/2015/sep/25/rufus-norris-first-national-theatre-season-interview.

———. 2018. Natasha Gordon Interview. *Independent*, 30 November. https://www.independent.co.uk/arts-entertainment/theatre-dance/features/natasha-gordon-interview-nine-night-trafalgar-studios-play-a8659091.html.

Davis, K. 2008. Intersectionality as Buzzword: A Sociology of Science Perspective on What Makes a Feminist Theory Successful. *Feminist Theory* 9 (1): 67–85.

Diamond, E., D. Varney, and C. Amich. 2017. *Performance, Feminism and Affect in Neoliberal Times*. London: Palgrave Macmillan.

Dolan, J. 2012 [1988]. *The Feminist Spectator as Critic*. Ann Arbor: University of Michigan Press.

Eddo-Lodge, R. 2018 [2017]. *Why I'm No Longer Talking to White People About Race*. London: Bloomsbury.

Eisenstein, Z.R. 1981. *The Radical Future of Liberal Feminism*. New York: Longman.

Evans, E. 2015. *The Politics of Third Wave Feminisms: Neoliberalism, Intersectionality, and the State in Britain and the US*. Basingstoke: Palgrave Macmillan.

Fisher, T. 2017. On the Performance of 'Dissensual Speech'. In *Performing Antagonism: Theatre, Performance and Radical Democracy*, ed. T. Fisher and E. Katsouraki, 187–207. London: Palgrave Macmillan.

Freeman, S. 1997. *Putting Your Daughters on the Stage: Lesbian Theatre from the 1970s to the 1990s*. London: Cassell.

Friedan, B. 2010 [1963]. *The Feminine Mystique*. London: Penguin.

Gardner, L. 2016. Emma Rice Is Right to Experiment at the Globe—Art Should Reinvent Not Replicate. *Guardian*, 28 September. https://www.theguardian.com/stage/theatreblog/2016/sep/28/emma-rice-shakespeares-globe-theatre-modern-audiences.

———. 2017. It's Time the UK's Top Theatre Committed to Gender Quotas. *The Stage*, 18 September. https://www.thestage.co.uk/opinion/2017/lyn-gardner-time-uks-top-theatres-committed-gender-quotas/.

———. 2019. Theatre's Class Ceiling. Digital Theatre+, 29 March. https://www.digitaltheatreplus.com/education/news/lyn-gardner-on-theatre-and-performance-theatres-class-ceiling.

Greig, D. 2017. *Aeschylus: The Suppliant Women*. London: Faber & Faber.

Grierson, J. 2017. British Theatre Bosses Condemn Sexual Harassment in the Industry. *Guardian*, 23 October. https://www.theguardian.com/stage/2017/oct/23/british-theatre-bosses-condemn-sexual-harassment-in-industry.

Hall, S. 1988. *The Hard Road to Renewal: Thatcherism and the Crisis of the Left*. London: Verso.

Hall, S., and B. Schwarz. 1988. State and Society, 1880–1930. In *Thatcherism and the Crisis of the Left: The Hard Road to Renewal*, S. Hall, 95–122. London: Verso.

Harris, R., and P.J. Larkham. 1999. Suburban Foundation, Form and Function. In *Changing Suburbs: Foundation, Form and Function*, ed. R. Harris and P.J. Larkham, 1–31. London: E & FN Spon.

Harrop, S. 2018. Greek Tragedy, Agonistic Space, and Contemporary Performance. *New Theatre Quarterly* 34 (2): 99–114.

Hemmings, C. 2011. *Why Stories Matter: The Political Grammar of Feminist Theory*. Durham: Duke University.

Hesford, V. 2013. *Feeling Women's Liberation*. Durham: Duke University.

Hesmondhalgh, J. 2019. *Julie Hesmondhalgh: A Working Diary*. London: Bloomsbury.

Heywood, L., and J. Drake. 1997. *Third Wave Agenda: Being Feminist, Doing Feminism*. Minneapolis: University of Minnesota Press.

Hollows, J. 2006. Can I Go Home Yet? Feminism, Post-feminism and Domesticity. In *Feminism in Popular Culture*, ed. J. Hollows and R. Moseley, 97–118. Oxford: Berg.

hooks, b. 1994. *Outlaw Culture: Resisting Representations*. London: Routledge.

Howard, E. 1965 [1902]. *Garden Cities of To-Morrow*, ed. F.J. Osborn. London: Faber.

Jones, O. 2011. *Chavs: The Demonization of the Working Class*. London: Verso.

Kennedy, H. 2018. *Eve Was Shamed: How British Justice Is Failing Women*. London: Chatto & Windus.

Kerbel, L. 2017. *All Change Please: A Practical Guide for Achieving Gender Equality in Theatre*. London: Nick Hern.

Kiraly, M., and M. Tyler, eds. 2015. *Freedom Fallacy: The Limits of Liberal Feminism*. Ballarat: Connor Court.

Labour Party. 2017. Acting Up Report: Labour's Inquiry into Access and Diversity in the Performing Arts. https://d3n8a8pro7vhmx.cloudfront.net/campaigncountdown/pages/1157/attachments/original/1502725031/Acting-Up-Report.pdf?1502725031.

Lansley, S., and J. Mack. 2015. *Breadline Britain: The Rise of Mass Poverty*. London: Oneworld.

Lee, V. 2019. *Emilia* Is Every Woman's Story—It's a Shared Experience. Interview with Saffron Coomber, Clare Perkins and Adelle Leonce. *Evening Standard*, 11 March. https://www.standard.co.uk/go/london/theatre/emilia-interview-saffron-coomber-adelle-leonce-clare-perkins-a4088091.html.

Love, C. 2013. Great Gala, But Where Were the Women Writers? *WhatsOnStage*, 4 November. https://www.whatsonstage.com/london-theatre/news/catherine-love-great-gala-but-where-were-the-women_32534.html.

Lovell, K. 2019. Emilia—A West End Show Which Delivers on Diversity. *Disability Arts Online*, 23 April. https://disabilityarts.online/magazine/opinion/emilia-a-west-end-show-which-delivers-on-diversity/.

Lovenduski, J., and V. Randall. 1993. *Contemporary Feminist Politics: Women and Power in Britain*. Oxford: Oxford University Press.

Lugones, M. 2003. *Pilgrimages/Peregrinajes: Theorizing Coalition Against Multiple Oppressions*. Lanham, MD: Rowman & Littlefield.

Lynch, K., J. Baker, and M. Lyons. 2009. *Affective Equality: Love, Care and Injustice*. Basingstoke: Palgrave Macmillan.

Mackay, F. 2015. *Radical Feminism: Feminist Activism in Movement*. Basingstoke: Palgrave Macmillan.

Malcolm, M.L. 2018. *Emilia*. London: Oberon.

———. 2019a. A Glimpse Inside with Morgan Lloyd Malcolm-Part 1. *View from the Outside*, 8 March. https://viewfromtheoutside.blog/2019/03/08/a-glimpse-inside-with-morgan-lloyd-malcolm-part-1/.

———. 2019b. A Glimpse Inside with Morgan Lloyd Malcolm-Part 2. *View from the Outside*, 10 March. https://viewfromtheoutside.blog/2019/03/10/a-glimpse-inside-with-morgan-lloyd-malcolm-part-2/.

McGowan, J. 2008. 'Dispute', 'Battle', 'Siege', 'Farce'?—Grunwick 30 Years On. *Contemporary British History* 22 (3): 383–406.

McMillan, J. 2016. Preview of *The Suppliant Women*. *Scotsman*, 27 September. http://www.scotsman.com/lifestyle/culture/theatre/preview-the-suppliant-women-at-the-royal-lyceum-1-4241294.

———. 2017. Interview with David Greig. *Scotsman*, 9 May. https://www.scotsman.com/arts-and-culture/theatre/theatre-interview-artistic-director-david-greig-talks-about-bringing-greater-diversity-to-the-royal-lyceum-s-programme-for-2017-18-1-4436329.

McRobbie, A. 2009. *The Aftermath of Feminism: Gender, Culture and Social Change*. London: Sage.
Minamore, B. 2018. 'We're Here!' The Black Playwrights Storming the West End. *Guardian*, 3 October. https://www.theguardian.com/stage/2018/oct/03/west-end-black-theatre-misty-arinze-kene-nine-night-natasha-gordon.
Mouffe, C. 2013. *Agonistics: Thinking the World Politically*. London: Verso.
———. 2018. *For a Left Populism*. London: Verso.
Ngai, S. 2007. *Ugly Feelings*. Cambridge, MA: Harvard University Press.
O'Brien, D. 2015. The Class Problem in British Acting: Talking at Camden People's Theatre. *Stratification and Culture Research Network*, 27 April. https://stratificationandculture.wordpress.com/2015/04/27/the-class-problem-in-british-acting-talking-at-camden-peoples-theatre/.
Okri, B. 2017. Grenfell Tower, June, 2017: A Poem. *Financial Times*, 23 June. https://www.ft.com/content/39022f72-5742-11e7-80b6-9bfa4c1f83d2.
Paget, D. 2009. The 'Broken Tradition' of Documentary Theatre and Its Continued Powers of Endurance. In *Get Real: Documentary Theatre Past and Present*, ed. A. Forsyth and C. Megson, 224–238. Basingstoke: Palgrave Macmillan.
Parish, S. 2018. We Must Break Down Barriers to Gender Parity. *The Stage*, 8 March. https://www.thestage.co.uk/opinion/2018/sphinx-theatres-sue-parrish-we-must-break-down-barriers-to-gender-parity/.
Pascal, J. 2018a. Review of *Emilia*. August. https://londongrip.co.uk/2018/08/emilia-shakespeares-globe-review-by-julia-pascal/.
———. 2018b. Women Are Being Excluded from the Stage. It's Time for Quotas. *Guardian*, 24 April. https://www.theguardian.com/commentisfree/2018/apr/24/women-theatre-quotas-stage-gender.
Raine, N. 2017. *Consent*. London: Nick Hern.
———. n.d. Nina Raine on *Consent*. National Theatre Blog. https://www.nationaltheatre.org.uk/blog/nina-raine-consent.
Rowbotham, S. 2019 [2000]. *Promise of a Dream: Remembering the Sixties*. London: Verso.
Royal Court Theatre. 2017. Code of Behaviour. https://royalcourttheatre.com/code-of-behaviour/.
Runcie, C. 2016. Review of *The Suppliant Women*. *Telegraph*, 13 October. https://www.telegraph.co.uk/theatre/what-to-see/the-suppliant-women-is-a-powerfully-feminist-timely-comment-on-t/.
Sadler, V. 2018. Theatre in Review: Challenges for Female Playwrights Continues. Victoria Sadler.com, 4 September. http://www.victoriasadler.com/2018-theatre-in-review-challenges-for-female-playwrights-continues/.
Segal, L. 2017. *Radical Happiness: Moments of Collective Joy*. London: Verso.

Seymour, R. 2016. *Corbyn: The Strange Rebirth of Radical Politics*. London: Verso.

Shellard, J. 2016. Mind the Gender Gap. *Purple Seven Theatre Magazine*, May, 41–42.

Shriver, L. 2010. Introduction. In *The Feminine Mystique*, B. Friedan, v–xi. London: Penguin.

Snow, G. 2015. Women 'Edge Towards Equality in Theatre'. *The Stage*, 10 December. https://www.thestage.co.uk/news/2015/gender-equality-moving-in-right-direction-claims-study/.

Spinoza, B. 1996. *Ethics*, trans. Edwin Curley. London: Penguin.

Strong-Boag, V., I. Dyck, K. England, and L. Johnson. 1999. What Women's Spaces? Women in Australian, British, Canadian and US Suburbs. In *Changing Suburbs: Foundation, Form and Function*, ed. R. Harris and P.J. Larkham, 168–186. London: E & FN Spon.

Taylor, P. 2018. Review of *Emilia*. *Independent*, 16 August. https://www.independent.co.uk/arts-entertainment/theatre-dance/reviews/emilia-shakespeares-globe-london-review-landmark-moment-for-the-globe-a8494911.html.

Thorpe, V. 2016. New Study Exposes 'Class Ceiling' That Deters Less Privileged Actors. *Guardian*, 27 February. https://www.theguardian.com/culture/2016/feb/27/class-ceiling-working-class-actors-study.

Topping, A. 2017. Theatre Director Max Stafford-Clark Was Ousted Over Inappropriate Behaviour. *Guardian*, 20 October. https://www.theguardian.com/stage/2017/oct/20/theatre-director-max-stafford-clark-was-ousted-over-inappropriate-behaviour.

Tripney, N. 2019. Michelle Terry: 'This Job Has Taught Me That Democracy Is Really Hard'. *The Stage*, 29 May. https://www.thestage.co.uk/features/interviews/2019/michelle-terry-this-job-has-taught-me-that-democracy-is-really-hard/.

Trueman, M. 2016. Review of *Escaped Alone*. *Variety*, 29 January. https://variety.com/2016/legit/reviews/escaped-alone-review-caryl-churchill-1201692064/.

TUC. 2017. 1 in 3 British BME Workers Have Been Bullied, Abused or Singled Out for Unfair Treatment, Finds TUC Poll. *TUC* Website, 13 September. https://www.tuc.org.uk/news/1-3-british-bme-workers-have-been-bullied-abused-or-singled-out-unfair-treatment-finds-tuc-poll.

Tyler, I. 2013. *Revolting Subjects: Social Abjection and Resistance in Neoliberal Britain*. London: Zed.

Wade, L. 2018. *Home, I'm Darling*. London: Oberon.

Walter, N. 1999. *The New Feminism*. London: Virago.

———. 2015 [2010]. *Living Dolls: The Return of Sexism*. London: Virago.

Wandor, M. 1981. *Understudies: Theatre and Sexual Politics*. London: Eyre Methuen.

———. 1986. *Carry On, Understudies: Theatre and Sexual Politics*. London: Routledge & Kegan Paul.

Weeks, K. 2014. Foreword. In *Women's Oppression Today: The Marxist/Feminist Encounter*, M. Barrett, ix–xix. London: Verso.

Wiegand, C. 2017. Ramin Gray of Actors Touring Company Faces Harassment Allegations. *Guardian*, 20 November. https://www.theguardian.com/stage/2017/nov/20/ramin-gray-actors-touring-company-harassment-allegations.

———. 2019. 'Let Them Roar': West End Stages First Baby-Friendly Performance. *Guardian*, 24 April. https://www.theguardian.com/stage/2019/apr/24/let-them-roar-west-end-stages-first-baby-friendly-performance.

Williams, R. 1973. *The Country and the City*. St. Albans, Herts: Paladin.

Wilmer, S.E. 2005. Introduction. In *Rebel Women: Staging Ancient Greek Drama Today*, ed. J. Dillon and S.E. Wilmer, xiii–xxv. London: Methuen.

Wilson, A. 2018 [1978]. *Finding a Voice: Asian Women in Britain*, 2nd ed., n.p. Daraja Press.

Woddis, C. 2018. Review of *Emilia*. *Woddisreviews*, 18 August. http://woddisreviews.org.uk/reviews/emilia/#more-3781.

Woodward, C. 2017. Interview with Ramin Gray. *Carl Woodward Blog*, 7 November. https://www.mrcarlwoodward.com/interview/atcs-ramin-gray-i-think-the-search-for-who-is-the-weinstein-of-british-theatre-is-an-honourable-search/.

Woolcock, N. 2018. University Lecturers to Strike as Students Sit Summer Exams. *The Times*, 9 March. https://www.thetimes.co.uk/article/university-lecturers-to-strike-as-students-sit-summer-exams-2jmmxlsbx.

Websites

Act for Change. https://www.act-for-change.com/.

Arts Emergency. https://arts-emergency.org/.

Common Theatre. https://commontheatre.co.uk/.

Panic! http://www.createlondon.org/panic/.

Purple Seven. https://purplesevenanalytics.com/.

Tonic Theatre. https://www.tonictheatre.co.uk/.

Unfinished Histories. https://www.unfinishedhistories.com/.

ERA 50:50. http://equalrepresentationforactresses.co.uk/.

Index

E. Aston, *Restaging Feminisms*,
https://doi.org/10.1007/978-3-030-40589-2

GPSR Compliance
The European Union's (EU) General Product Safety Regulation (GPSR) is a set of rules that requires consumer products to be safe and our obligations to ensure this.

If you have any concerns about our products, you can contact us on

ProductSafety@springernature.com

In case Publisher is established outside the EU, the EU authorized representative is:

Springer Nature Customer Service Center GmbH
Europaplatz 3
69115 Heidelberg, Germany

www.ingramcontent.com/pod-product-compliance
Ingram Content Group UK Ltd.
Pitfield, Milton Keynes, MK11 3LW, UK
UKHW021617180625
459763UK00013B/41

* 9 7 8 3 0 3 0 4 0 5 8 8 5 *